# The Courage to Believe:
## *How Human Life May Flourish*

Roy J. Enquist

Hansen-McMenamy Books, LLC
www.hansenmcmenamybooks.com

For Mia

© 2009 by Roy J. Enquist

Cover design by Jordan Taafe-McMenamy
Edited by Marsha Hansen

All rights reserved. No part of this book may be reproduced or transmitted in any form or by any means, electronic or mechanical, including photocopying, recording, or by any information storage or retrieval system, without written permission from Hansen-McMenamy Books, LLC, except for inclusion or quotation in a review.

Library of Congress Cataloging-in-Publication Data

Enquist, Roy J.

The Courage To Believe: *How Human Life May Flourish*

Includes bibliographical references and index.

International Standard Book Number: 978-0-9822655-2-9

Manufactured in the U.S.A.

Hansen-McMenamy Books, LLC          El Paso, Texas

**Special First Edition**

# Contents

## Foreword by Nicholas Beale

| | | |
|---|---|---|
| Chapter 1 | The Confusions and Possibilities of Faith | 9 |
| Chapter 2 | What's Real? | 25 |
| Chapter 3 | What Does God Have to Do With It? | 42 |
| Chapter 4 | The First Gift | 51 |
| Chapter 5 | The Jesus Question | 88 |
| Chapter 6 | From Moses to Martin | 105 |
| Chapter 7 | On Being Well and Being Well Connected | 125 |
| Notes | | 147 |

## Foreword

## By Nicholas Beale

Trust is the lifeblood of a successful society. Love requires trust. Raising children requires trust. Education depends on trust. Successful economies depend enormously on trust. Healthy social orders are built on trust. Whenever we trust in another human being or human institution there is always the possibility that we will be let down, but we invest in trust and risk trusting in order to experience community, growth, and fulfillment. The philosopher of science Michael Polyani wrote his great book *Personal Knowledge* "to explain how I can commit myself to what I believe to be true, knowing that it might be false." Trust is ultimately a matter of faith.

In *The Courage to Believe,* Roy Enquist explores, with eloquence and insight, many aspects of what faith is about and what it means for us as individuals and in society. Reading through it, I have highlighted hundreds of phrases and sentences on which to reflect further. Among these are his essential idea - that faith is an adventure, that faith is not just a system of beliefs: it is consciously living in a web of connectedness. In drawing out these connections, he writes that "marriage, politics, economics and ecology are all grounded in the capacity to trust and be trusted ... How can this be any less true of the life of faith?" How indeed? This capacity to trust God is nourished by our participation in holiness. Enquist notes that "Jesus has insisted that God's holiness is fundamentally God's love... Faith is the holy at work in us, fully accepting us."

God's work of love requires our loving cooperation. However as Enquist rightly points out, we live in a cultural environment and a public society which can make this difficult.

"Self-destructive behaviors, both individually and socially, are both pervasive and popular in contemporary society. We chiefly experience this destructiveness in terms of a hostility, and alienation from others as well as from ourselves and from God."

By contrast, when we live in a web of justice and connectedness with our neighbours and with God, we transcend selfish individualism and the pursuit of material gain. Paradoxically, a society where individuals are not simply out for all they can get is more likely to succeed economically than one where there are no restraints on personal greed other than the risk of getting caught. It is noteworthy that one of the global banks that has fared best in the present crisis and without government help is HSBC. Chairman of HSBC, Stephen Green, is a Christian priest. His recent book *Good Value* is a deep and eloquent appeal to people in business to find their moral and spiritual roots. His book is very much consonant with the messages of *The Courage to Believe*, messages of hope for God to work through us and in us, whether we are considering the economy, the environment, or our most basic relationships.

This book challenges one to ask, who obstructs the work of God in us? Is it true that we moderns are experts at obscuring the Holy? For some people, the idea that Science has in some sense disproved religion is one such obstacle to be overcome. Leading scientists like Francis Collins and John Polkinghorne have worked hard and successfully to dispel this misconception. In 1997, I was serving with John Polkinghorne on the Committee that advised the Church of England on Science, Medicine and Technology and we were beginning work on the Ethical and Spiritual Implications of the Internet. After 10 years we had a treasure-trove of questions from people who wrote to us, and we thought it would be helpful to build a book, *Questions of Truth*, around some of the more interesting ones. By 2009 John and I could write in that book, without fear of reasonable contradiction, "It is logically possible that belief in God is mistaken—but it is certainly not a "delusion."... There is no real conflict between science and Christianity.

Of course it takes decades for popular culture to catch up with reality. Lazy thinking and vested interests still lead to claims that there is "warfare between Science and Religion" but almost no serious philosopher or historian of science would accept this, and few first-rank scientists do. ." Though *The Courage to Believe* treats many different elements of faith, I was struck by Roy Enquist's rich contribution to the conversation on science and religion in Chapter Four. He makes tremendous strides in further dispelling the notion of a conflict. However, even with many obstacles cleared, developing a living relationship with God, in which his holiness and love work more and more powerfully within us, is both demanding and daunting.

When speaking of the courage to believe, Enquist encourages us to see ourselves as embodied participants in a set of wider communities. Of course the individual's relationship with God is of paramount importance, but God calls us into a community where we have to love God with all our soul, mind and strength and where we love our neighbour as ourselves. The prophets repeatedly call us to see this love, and God's justice, in both personal and social terms. Enquist commends "the variety of attempts to develop a robust theology of a public church" and points out that the world that God so loved was never a world devoid of public culture. One of the most encouraging recent developments in the constructive dialogue between science and religion has been the shared work on developing a deeper awareness and consensus on climate change and the care of the Creation, with for example leading scientists like Jim McCarthy and EO Wilson taking the lead in initiating deep dialogue with evangelical leaders. As Enquist says:

*It is only when we begin to see how demanding that loving one's neighbor as oneself has become in our increasingly complex world, that we begin to appreciate we are also facing an energy crisis. Where do we get the energy as communities and persons to address the kinds of challenges just cited? Whatever we mean by spirit, most of us would agree that we certainly will need a lot of it if we are going to get anywhere.*

All over the world, people are discovering the courage to believe – the recent book *God is Back* gives a fascinating global perspective on this. Repressive atheism is in global decline, though as Haydn noted so beautifully in *The Creation* "despairing, cursing rage attends their rapid fall." Meanwhile, books like this one provide us with rich food for thought on the adventure of faith in the 21$^{st}$ Century, for indeed:

*Life has a logos, a logic that is utterly greater than itself, a logos within which one is able to live into the gift of an abundant life.*

## CHAPTER ONE

### *The Confusions and Possibilities of Faith*

It may seem odd to begin a public conversation about the confusions and possibilities of faith on a personal note. After all, aren't the social implications of religion, good or bad, more pressing? Perhaps that's where we should begin. Or maybe not.

Religion always has had both public and personal significance. That's what helps make it so confusing. The social profile of religion seems easier and less embarrassing to access. But unless we can recognize up-front that our conversation about religion has personal resonance, we will have inevitably prejudged and diminished its meaning. So, why try to avoid getting personal?

You may have noticed that when we talk about social issues, especially important ones, we may want to try to avoid having to recognize the influence of our biases. That seems true whether you're a friend or enemy of religion. In fact, it's likely that the more controversial an issue is, the greater impact it will have on our personal perspective. That's obviously true when we're talking about the big ones: religion, politics, or sexuality. One difficulty in getting started to have a useful discussion about God lies in our natural reluctance to acknowledge the need to reflect on the strengths and weaknesses of our assumptions about religion. Being in denial that each person is a unique subject and not just one more object in a larger class makes matters much worse.

I can't remember when I first was told anything about God. Probably it was in early childhood when my mother taught me to say each night, "Now I lay me down to sleep. I pray thee Lord . . ." I could not have said so then, of course, but at that moment I had just learned that basically religion is action, an act of communication. Looking back, I see that an infant's prayer carries with it the preposterous promise that it is possible for even a very small child to be in instant communication with the primordial, enduring, transcendent, holy, creative energy that pervades all reality. The halting adjectives came, of course, much later. What's remarkable is that billions of children do take this personally. They too, get to give this infinite creativity a very personal name: Father.

The assumption that I could get into personal contact with sublime holiness, however dimly perceived, was not a surprise. Since my natural father had died (encephalitis) late in the year before I was born, wasn't it about time that I could be told how I could get into touch with someone who is stronger than death? Should not a child be permitted to think that getting this amazing good news is a part of what it means to be welcomed into the world?

Not much more was said about religion back then until, one day, my third grade girl friend invited me to go with her to Sunday School at Trinity Church. I remember that when we got there, it seemed like a very crowded place. I wondered, "What's going on here? Who are all these noisy people?" How was I to know that quite by chance it happened to be Easter Day? For that matter, what's Easter?

Looking back, I now see that what I got week after following week, was a trip to a strange Norway in which everyone sort of spoke English. That could prove promising: a free trip to Europe every week, not as tourist, but as a pilgrim. Every week: kids and teachers from all over town, chorales and chanting, a white and gold altar with a huge reredos framing a painting of the ascension, fourteen real candles aflame, and, at the heart of it all, a community mostly steeped in a piety recently transplanted from what was then Europe's poor northlands. Every week I got to explore my family's spiritual history as an evangelical catholic Viking—even though, as they constantly reminded me, "You're not a Norwegian." I, of course, was not disappointed to know they were right. Looking back now, I see now how fragile that rich heritage would soon become.

I've often wondered why I took all this seriously. It's easy for adults to misjudge the faith of children: "You can get little kids to believe anything." But actually, it is not so easy to understand the faith of children. A first century rabbi was not well received when he noted that adults need to find out how to become as spiritually alert as their children. In my own case, these many years later, it has gradually become clear why faith may have become such a big deal for me. Actually, it was not a matter of preserving an ethnic memory. Such ties often can be an enemy of faith, as the history of religions has repeatedly shown. Tribal ties commonly get in the way of faith—as that first century rabbi also pointed out.

So what meanings for faith did I discover in my childhood?

- *Faith is an adventure. For a child it's a way of asking questions about strange mysteries. It's a discovery of a new world—a world that enables you to see that the world you experience each day really is deeply unsatisfactory. (Don't tell anyone you found that out. They won't approve.)*
- *Faith is being safe, secure, not being afraid. Faith overcomes fear. If you really know what's going on around you, you could name a lot of things to be afraid of. Why do grown-ups think that being a kid is easy—especially if you are living in tough times and there are a lot more bad guys out there than are really needed?*
- *Faith means being connected. This is how it works: you don't have to be afraid because if you stay connected to your father, he'll be there for you. It's really a matter of trust, of being willing to trust So faith means you are never alone. Coeur d'Alene was a small town, all right, and your family was very fragile, but you're not really alone. There's always someone to talk to even when you forget to do that. Faith means you're connected to another One whether a lot of people are around or not–or care or not. And (here's the big deal), since you're not really alone, its quite possible that you will be able to get a much better future than you, by yourself, can even begin to imagine.*
- *Faith also means you need to know what you believe. That's the hard part. Of course, you should believe what the Bible teaches. Unfortunately, there seems to be no agreement among the grown-ups as to what the Bible does teach. Some say God wrote the Bible so it's a perfect book even though it's very confusing and seems to have a lot of contradictions. Some say*

*that there are some important ministers in Europe someplace who are able to understand God perfectly. But, when you check it out, it turns out that for a very long time they haven't agreed on a lot of important things. Conclusion: A lot of grown-ups have ideas about religion (pro or con) that don't make any sense at all. So faith means you have to put up with this. It means you have to figure out what you should believe. And that's a problem because who's good enough or smart enough to do that? Bottom line: Belief is an important aspect of faith, but belief always involves thinking and asking questions (and that involves doubt) which gets us back to where we started: faith is a venture.*

There is no way to quantify these aspects of faith or to exclude others not mentioned. But a childhood without access to at least these few has been spiritually abused. A child quickly notices that an adult who doesn't understand why trust and being connected, being safe, being able to ask questions, and being able to seek out adventure are all necessary for growing up is not someone who is going to be of much help when you need it.

The concepts a child uses in trying to understand faith will change from time to time. That probably has always been true: change is inevitable. But in today's world the rate of change has accelerated dramatically—not only because the cultures which shape our experience of life are rapidly changing, but because a dynamic faith is compelled to challenge them. In the twenty-first century, controversy about the significance of faith has increased significantly. Adding to the problem is trying to understand what all this has to do with religion. Here is a short list of eleven issues:

## What Does Faith have to do with Religion?

Faith and religion are related but by no means synonymous. It is necessary to note their difference as well as their relatedness. It's commonly said, "I'm not really religious, but I am a spiritual person." Usually that distinction is intended to mean something like "Of course I have faith; I just don't follow any organized religion." Actually the prophetic tradition says much the same thing—and does so much more powerfully. For our purposes here we can think of faith primarily as trust. Being able to trust and to be trusted are essential for human life. But religions claiming to represent some transcendent, ultimate meaning are usually careful not to confuse that claim with their own social institutions. The religious name for that confusion is idolatry.

But faith and religion are not mutually exclusive. Very different social structures can nurture communities of faith. The Greek Orthodox Church in Jerusalem understands itself to be the Body of Christ. So too does a Baptist congregation in Iraq. The people in both of these assemblies understand themselves to be connected to God through Christ in the Spirit. There is no empirical way to determine whether they are or are not. Sociology helps us understand the character of these religious institutions, but the actual dynamics of faith expressed in them are quite another matter. Faith, believers agree, is the work of the Spirit. But the Spirit is like the wind, we have been told. You can not see it, but you can only see what it can do.

In modern times, however, faith and religion are often confused. This blurring could be a strategic move on the part of self-described non-believers since any social institution, including religion of course, is an easy target. But the secularization of the West is deeper than that. For more than a century now there has been a consensus among major intellectuals that the world is moving inexorably "to a time of no religion at all." Whether institutions of religion persist, society itself will have become functionally godless.

More recently, however, doubt as to the truth of that expectation has begun to seep in. What world, people of faith began to ask, are they talking about? Who gets to decide that faith cannot be embodied in fallible human structures? However difficult, if not impossible, it may be to measure faith-as-trust, in practice, religion as a social phenomenon has not disappeared. Maybe atheism is the established faith among some elites, but religion itself seems to be flourishing across the globe. Neither religion (as a cultural phenomenon) nor faith (as a basic element in self-awareness) seems to be in danger of disappearing.

## A Bit of Background

It is true, of course, that the traditions of atheism, both intellectual and non-reflective, are very much with us. The anti-religious legacy of Feuerbach, Nietzsche, Marx, and Freud have proven widely influential. Their cultural achievement, however, has proven a huge embarrassment. Where is the liberation of humanity which they believed that their "anti-theological" work would generate? Philosophers of religion, to be sure, still take this important quartette seriously, and serious theologians still seek to co-opt their work. But the old thrill is gone. Is it because whatever their differences, all four of these men bought in on the left-wing Hegelian assumption that since God can not be shown to be an object, religion must be a delusion? Had none of them been told that the first commandment in the Decalogue absolutely condemns the universal attempt to try to make God into an object? How could none of them have not noticed that? Did Marx skip confirmation class the day his pastor discussed idolatry? Well, even creative people can't be expected to notice everything. Less excusable are modern intellectuals who assume that somebody, somewhere, must have proved that the secularist arguments of the left wing Hegelians were true. But who actually did that? Do we just have to take that on faith that someone did?

## It Really Doesn't Matter

It may be that it is the unreflective atheists who are more significant than the philosophers. There certainly are many more of them. It is possible for people today never to think about religion at all—one way or another. Unreflective atheism may simply be religious indifference. Since religion seems to be either boring or dangerous it's best to leave it alone. Anyhow, religion is unimportant, it doesn't matter.

Well, maybe. But as sociologists of religion have pointed out, religion isn't quite so easy to get rid of. Modern culture created a wide variety of new "transcendence-free religions," movements that foster devotion to popular secular values, i.e. consumerism, chauvinism and other forms of political extremism, racism, sexism, hedonism, etc. While the secular substitutes for religion can inspire both loyalty and fanaticism, they also inherit the critique that all religions face: What are their consequences for their true believers and for all of us on Earth?

**Leave Religion Out of It**

Since religion in a pluralistic society is inherently controversial, the temptation to minimize its role in public life has proven hard to resist. In the United States teaching "about religion" in the public schools, though repeatedly affirmed by the Supreme Court, has become politically impossible in most places. But surely the Court is right. Since the American peoples, from before there was a United States, have been deeply engaged with a variety of religions, to review their colorful historical narrative with its religions excised is to falsify the record. A non-prejudicial review of the American story cannot but expose the presence of persisting spiritualities—whether conveyed or repressed by religious institutions. Why, then, the need to hide religion's roles? One reason: Prophetic religion, so vividly displayed in both the Old and New Testaments dares deliver uncompromising messages of divine condemnation on tribes, nations, and empires because of their opposition to any transcendent justice. "Well then, love it or leave it," the patriots insist. "The message of an ancient foreign religion cannot be used as a guide for a modern society," academics argue. "Religion must be trumped by more important interests—chiefly economic and cultural." Intellectual atheism does not need to mount an attack on the divine. Unreflective atheism will do the heavy lifting. It will simply reinforce our loyalties to what is beyond criticism, the values of our own tribe.

## Two Twentieth Century Social Experiments

The social consequences of intellectual atheism in recent Western history deserve more attention than they usually receive. The major religious experiment of the twentieth century was to demonstrate the political implications of the theological thesis: God is dead. The laboratory was not the ivied tower beloved by the academics. It was a popular movement, much like a religion itself. The sparks first flew in Europe, but then, like wild fire, the conflagration went global. The thesis had first been proposed in Western Europe, but the communist revolution swiftly moved east to Russia and again still farther east—all the way to the Pacific. The revolution bloodily morphed into empires and new anti-religious political religions were quickly imposed. This was not an urbane atheism, a mere philosophical project. This was a war against the cultural values of millions of people. In the USSR, all the clergy of the nation's largest Protestant Church had been killed before WWII. Why? Clergy suspected of Reformation sympathies must be eliminated so that a new humankind may emerge unfettered by the superstition, injustice and oppression supposedly characteristic of the fascist West. This cry was not an argument. It was the proclamation of a secular hope now engaged in seeking the approval of the unreflective masses.

It is not true that unreflective atheism always leads to a particularly deadly form of communism. But what have we learned from one of the most significant social experiments in all of human history, one based on the belief that religion is humanity's mortal enemy, a belief that requires the murder of millions? Perhaps it is true that when God is dead everything is possible. Everything, it seems, except obedience to the law to love one's neighbor as oneself.

But history, as you may have noticed, did not come to an end after all. Since its earliest days, the central religious feast for Christians has been Easter, the celebration of the resurrection. In the twenty-first century, large choirs in Moscow's churches again sing, "He is risen." But if you look farther east you will see an even more surprising consequence of an importation of Western atheism. According to Professor John Yeh-HanYieh of Virginia Theological Seminary, the 700,000 Chinese Christians at the end of WWII have now grown to forty-six million  Perhaps by the end of this century we shall  have a Chinese pope.

The other European experiment in hostility to ancient religion rose not from the cultural left but from the right, from the *fear* of communism. The fascisms developed in Spain, Italy and Germany did not have the honesty of the left. Religion was not to be banished. It was to be exploited to serve the new political religions championed by secular conservatives. The argument:

True religion is not to be found in church or synagogue. The religion of the future is to be the nation. The state, not the church, is the proper instrument for the ordering of public life. That is why the internationalism of the Roman Catholic Church and the individualism of Protestantism must be overcome. The best strategy: co-option. Both faith communities, albeit in different ways, threaten the supremacy of the state; they weaken the state in its crucial  life-and-death struggle against communism. It would be foolish to follow the communist model by abolishing them. These major forms of Western Christianity can be of service to the fascist cause if they are forced to assume a supportive role in the struggle. It is not necessary, of course, that all believers oppose fascism, but it is crucial that that their major leaders do. Why shouldn't the papacy be willing to support the fascist movement in its struggle against godless communism?  Why shouldn't Protestant clergy, liberal as well as conservative, see that national fascism can be their bulwark against the godless left?

Of course, not everyone could be seduced into giving this project at least tacit support. But many did. Whether out of *naïveté* or cowardice the consequences have been the same. Their caving into fascism's demands exposed the slow, obscured decay of the Christian legacy in Europe, a new wounding from which it appears it may never recover.

## Why Faith is Not Religion

What does all this twentieth century history have to do with the relation of faith to religion today? Much, or little, depending on what the word *faith* means. When faith is classically perceived to be the act of being apprehended by a divine reality that transcends all things (including all religious structures), it is quite possible to critique or even reject any particular form of religion. Putting it somewhat paradoxically, one can say that even though a particular experience of faith typically arises and is sustained within a social setting that has been shaped by a constellation of religious practices, people of faith understand themselves to be connected absolutely to a transcendence not subject to human control. When this dialectic is ignored, philosophy and sociology may still be possible, but not theology.

Even small children may discover that believing in God is deeply associated with being able to feel safe and unafraid, having the confidence to venture forth to meet scary challenges, to know that you are deeply connected not just to your family but to everything in the whole wide world. Being able to figure out how believing all this is not easy. It can take more than a life time. But it's not impossible and it's not hard to see that it's a lot more interesting, more promising, than the alternatives: just give up, run away, accept that you have to be captive to fear, to isolation, or to thinking that you're the only one that matters.

## Faith and History

Theology, at least in the biblical tradition, seems to make its difficult task much more so by requiring that faith has to be grounded in history. What could be more obvious than that the historical record doesn't give much evidence that God is doing a pretty good job of running the world? But then biblical theology is not in the business of summarizing the obvious. Its job is to resist moral complacency and religious superficiality. Its task is to show that being grounded in history does not mean being confined to it. Defensive, self-serving, chauvinist readings of history are a dime a dozen and continue to sell well. They typically celebrate a nation's self interest as though that were the same as its self identity. This sort of national pride is not absent from the earliest strata of the biblical narrative, but was mercilessly repudiated by the prophetic tradition beginning with Amos which goes on to saturate the New Testament. What was it that made this perspective possible? How can mere historical reflection be both a subversive judgment and a transformative resource for a whole people? Can that miracle be repeated?

When it is done today it recognizes that the Bible focuses not on the typical, the orderly, the normative, but on the unconventional, the extraordinary, the incommensurate. Of course, every decent rationalist has to abhor this kind of approach to history. If history is a social science, how can that be otherwise? Is not what is typical is what is normative? Do we not have to assume that our understanding of history must be bound to such supposed rationalities as the relation of cause and effect? But what if the truth of the matter is bound up in an undetermined future, a horizon that has not already been experienced? What if the meaning of the life of the reader of these lines lies not in what has been set, settled and established, but in what is yet to be?

### Is Biblical History Credible?

There is another important problem that troubles professional historians. The minimalist party asks whether the Bible is a book of history at all. They "categorize the biblical account of the history of Israel as fiction, the product of religious propaganda from a much later date." [1] A book, much larger than the one you are now reading, would be required to trace the issues raised in the pros and cons of the minimalist position. The debate should be encouraged. It does not, however, eclipse a discussion of the meaning of the Bible. When we speak of biblical history, we should not imply that its writers were able to work with the methods and tools employed by historians in the twenty-first century. For that matter, the great historians of the nineteenth were not able to do that either. Obsolescence is as common in the academy as on the assembly line. It is enough for today's historian to note that ancient texts freely employed a wide variety of current literary forms which are now considered as out-of-date. The question of historicity in the Bible is the question of how much we today can regard as fact and how much as fiction. [2]

We today do not regard etiological stories as fact. They are, however, invaluable as sources for understanding the cultures of the people who told and recorded them. Both Testaments are rich in profoundly significant poetry: Genesis 1, Job, the Psalms, I Corinthians 13 come quickly to mind. Stories about Jonah, the Good Samaritan, the Wise and Foolish Virgins, are brilliant and enduring pieces of fiction. Why does the eroticism of the Song of Solomon or the apocalyptic texts in I Thessalonians and Revelation not evoke the historian's protest, "This is mere fantasy, only fiction, not history?" The Bible is a library rich in what the ancients experienced as history as well as much which is poetry, fiction, philosophy—all conditioned by the canons and resources which its writers were obliged to employ. Their work too is a part of sacred history. A library notable for its moral seriousness, its record of ancient wisdom, its discoveries of transcendent mystery will continue to serve as the decisive literary authority for communities of faith. It is not the task of the research scholar to compel anyone to believe that God is active in the historical past. That takes nothing less than the Spirit of God. [3]

**Faith and the Bible**

Our final task in this chapter, then, is to ask whether there is any congruence between a child's elemental faith and an ancient library whose texts are increasingly unfamiliar to people today? Is it possible, at least, to find rudimentary answers?

Faith, in the first instance, is not a system of beliefs but an act of venture. Clement of Rome in CE 95 was very fond of an anonymous, elegant, highly literary sermon which later Christians mistakenly attributed to Paul.[4] We today know it as the Letter to the Hebrews. Chapter eleven is an extended meditation on the meaning of faith. Strange to say, this major Christian document does not cite the apostolic community as an exemplar of faith. Rather, it is a group of Israelite heroes who are praised: Abel, Enoch, Noah, Abraham, Moses, Gideon, Barak, Samson, Jephthah, David, Samuel, the prophets and "women (who) received their dead." It clearly is number four, Abraham, who is the decisive figure. For it was he who set out, not knowing where he was going...to the city that has foundations, whose architect and builder is God. (His descendants will be) as many as the stars of heaven and as the innumerable grains of sand by the seashore (even though they are but) strangers and foreigners on the earth.[5]

The literary beauty of the Greek text is not completely obscured by English translations. But what is especially notable is that intellectually sophisticated, learned sermons were being preached to Gentiles in first century Italy in a time of persecution encouraging them to look all the way back to Abraham for a model for the life of faith they would need. Abraham had ventured forth into the unknown; God blessed him wonderfully; God will do that for them who have that kind of faith.

## How Faith Functions Today

Faith is not a system of beliefs, but a prophylactic against fear. The world for most children at most times in most places has been a scary place. Fear is an appropriate and rational response to a destructive environment. Unfortunately, fear also can be overwhelming and destructive. Rationality is wonderful. It is often, however, impotent in the face of fear. Of course, by fear we do not refer to the somewhat archaic use of the word to identify awesomeness, profound respect, reverence, deep humility before majesty. We refer rather to its strong modern sense as fright, panic, dread, terror, profound anxiety. We are talking about politics, economics, warfare, various pathologies, and cheap entertainment. None of these was unknown in antiquity. But it's likely that the increasing power of modern technology and industry will increase rather than diminish their range. That gloomy prospect can only increase the demand for robust avatars of faith which can show what it means to meet fear head on.

What does that have to do with us now? Notice how the powers of fear are being newly employed. Is the American response to 9/11 primarily a desire for revenge or fealty to fear or both? Why was it so easy to herd the public, like sheep, into believing (!) that rushing into preemptive war, full of shock and awe, would both banish our fear and deliver sweet revenge? Perhaps it was not all about oil after all.

Engagement with fear, in the modern and ancient senses of the word, figures prominently in both Testaments. Their writers tell of us of a time when the Earth itself will melt away. They speak of thieves who come at night. A brutal world empire is doomed, a bloody whore who has been devouring all in her way. Preoccupation with fear in this sense had been exactly appropriate for Judeans facing the advance of Babylonian armies to Jerusalem and again for Christians slated for martyrdom in Rome.

The Bible is mostly intended for adults' eyes. But even children may need to be prepared to face the monsters that invade their worlds. If the secularists believe that faith is not enough for every encounter, they may well be right. But how does a refusal to let children get access to transcendent faith help them? Do we, somehow, expect our children to be precocious Stoics? How does that differ from requiring African children to be precocious soldiers?

Faith in the first instance is not a system of beliefs. It is consciously living into a web of connectedness. A very great English philosopher once opined that religion is what one does with one's solitude. He may have been right, 5% right. An even greater Augustinian monk (in influence, at least) held that every individual must die alone. He may have been right too: 1% right. But Paul wrote, "Whether we live, or whether we die, we are the Lord's." [6] That's undoubtedly closer to the mark. An infant's very survival is dependent on an instinctive identification with a caregiver. Without another one in your life, you will not make it. In fact, while we are urged to note that life begins before birth, we need to note what is far more important: life begins long before conception. We are constituted by our connections.

How can one learn to think about anything if one has no access to communication with others? How can one flourish if there is no one to manage the supply of milk, the magical disappearance of feculence? Maybe mommy is everyone's first god. Who can hope to make it without her? How incidental, it may seem, is having a father. How hard, but how necessary, it will become to move on some day from these immediate gods.

**Faith and Ecology**

It seems likely that early peoples were more profoundly aware of their connection to the natural world than are people in later cultures. They characteristically understood that world as a place pervaded by spirits. The Bushmen of the Kalahari, the *Shintoists* at Nara, the Pueblos and the Apaches in America know that. Their religions differ from each another. But religion typically claims to make connections available for people at every level of the environment. Religion deeply underscores connections between human beings and the animal kingdom: we are all utterly dependent on an environment we have not made and do not really control. The ecological disasters now increasing in virulence are a graphic demonstration of the rapacious power of secularism's robust agent, global commerce. They surely are not the work of religion.

A major task for the religious communities and their theologians is how to revive the biblical insistence on the inner connectedness of all life as the primordial creative act of divine goodness. How can people be alerted to the claim that, as the neo-Augustinians tirelessly insist, "God is in, with, and under all things?" The modern project which requires the exploitation of the earth for the financial gain and comfort of a privileged minority is the new face of original sin. To exercise dominion over the creation in the biblical sense is to prize the goodness with which it is divinely invested. It is to care for it and nurture it as faithful agents of the source of all goodness, the *dominus* over all. Today's urgent moral task is to prioritize the significance of human connectedness to all life. The indispensable moral agent for all forms of connectedness is trust. If this seems like so much feckless tree hugging, consider these three seemingly non-religious issues:

- For pragmatic reasons, economists insist that access to credit is the basis of the global economic system. Credit is possible only when they who have financial resources can trust potential borrowers—and vice versa. When trust or confidence depart, the economy shuts down. Trust is indispensible.

- When nations and tribes within nations are no longer able to trust each other, diplomacy is replaced by war and terror. War is dramatic and enduringly trust—trust in the potential enemy. Peace is hard.

- In the traditional rites of marriage, the couple wishing to be wed are required at the beginning of the service to state publicly that they will be faithful to each other as long as both shall live. Marriage has many meanings, of course, but without a clear commitment to faithfulness, to a life of mutual trust, the service cannot go forward. This is not a ritual formality. Without it the rite is a travesty—and worse.

Thus, marriage, politics, economics and ecology are all grounded in the capacity to trust and to be trusted. How can that be any less true for the life of faith?

Faith cannot be reduced to a construct of beliefs. It is an act, an act of venture, confidence, caution, trust and connectedness which compels us to think about what our life means. This task is difficult but not impossible. What is impossible to accept is the notion that finite, flawed believers will ever reach such mastery of knowledge that they can claim to have constructed a perfect, final system of religious truths. That is not only impossible, it is the arrogance of intellectual idolatry and thus absolutely sinful. What is possible, and increasingly necessary, is our work in art, literature, politics, psychology and, not least of all, theology—that labors to show how a faith shaped by a love of God and neighbor is the good news that enables sinners actually to live as children of God.

## CHAPTER TWO

## *What's Real?*

"What's real?" For centuries religious thinkers, East and West, have searched for answers. The great religions of India, for example, have offered brilliant and complex responses: How can anyone not notice that all life (including one's own) is driven relentlessly by myriad forces of change? Surely, what endures is the changeless, eternal Brahman–"God," if you will. It is the task of religion to show us mortals how we may escape being caught in the trap of time, how we can finally be absorbed into, be made one with, the eternal, changeless Brahman, beyond time and space. Salvation is release from the trap.

Even in the less reflective West, does not everyone, whether religious or not, have to notice that we are all, inevitably, captives of change? Of course, in the short run, as most teenagers will tell you, change is what we want. Yes, of course. But, isn't it also true that in the long run, it will kill you?

Religious poets in the West have often thought about this. In eighteenth century England, Isaac Watts hauntingly expressed his sense of the essential pathos of human mortality:

> **Time, like an ever-rolling stream,**
> **Bears all its sons away;**
> **They fly forgotten, as a dream**
> **Dies at the opening day.** [1]

Are we then as ephemeral as dreams, we daughters and sons of time? A century later, Henry F. Lyte seemed to say so:

> **Swift to its close ebbs out life's little day.**
> **Earth's joy grow dim,**
> **Its glories pass away.**
> **Change and decay in all around I see . . .**

Decay in all around one surely can see, but is that all that there is? Lyte thought not. It should not be impossible to connect to the One who does not decay.

**O thou who changest not,
Abide with me.** [2]

It has seemed obvious to many, East and West, that that which ultimately matters, which endures, is that which is most real. What is transitory can only be of limited value. What endures is what is most truly real. It is the passing of time that makes a mess of everything.

But just as it looks that we, East and West, may finally have come to a consensus, a spiritual consensus in fact, we hit a brick wall. True, we are mortal creatures imbedded in time and space. But is that the only issue? Perhaps we need to explore the meaning of our mortality more carefully. Time is inescapable, to be sure. But does that make it an enemy?

Being aware that one is mortal can be a needed wake-up call. Facing the stubborn reality of one's mortality is a part of honest self-awareness. Of course, it can also be a deeply disturbing threat to one's sense of identity. But even in that case it could also serve as a station on the path to a deeper maturity.

Since world religions have typically focused on the desire to flee the temporal, to seek the eternal, it may come as a surprise to discover that the Bible does not do this. It does not begin with a meditation on the nature of eternity, the realm of the non-temporal. It begins with a word event, *dabar*, an explosion of events, all set in solemn, stately, if awkward, sequence. This creative Hebrew redaction of an older Babylonian tradition inspired Christians at the end of the first century to come up with another update: John's Gospel which began by echoing the first words of the Hebrew Bible, " In the beginning when God created" with a slight, but profound change: " In the beginning God communicated." [3]

These Hebrew and Greek texts presuppose that an event, something that happens in time, even time itself, does not have to be regarded as a trap. Who knows whether it is impossible for transcendence to invade time? These narratives explore what it means to believe that God is the creator of time, that time is the God-given context for the narrative of a good and godly creation.

Well before these beliefs were formulated, the Hebrew people had claimed that their own beginnings as a unique people rested on an event in time, the event of their liberation from bondage in Africa. This people claimed that as slaves of imperial Egypt they had encountered a God who had challenged them with the unlikely claim that they could be freed. How is this possible? Because divine justice demands it. The holy was henceforth to be experienced not as a transcendence that undergirds a mighty empire but rather boldly acts to defy it. Holiness comes from a realm far different from an imperial system that feeds on the slavery of immigrants. Holiness challenges slaves to act for justice and to embody it themselves.

This dubious vision was not helped when it turned out that its first advocate was a murderer bearing an Egyptian name. What was that all about? It should not be surprising that this Moses was initially reluctant to commit himself to the dangerous notion that the holy can evoke and validate profoundly subversive behavior. How can this be in a world in which holiness essentially meant stability? How can holiness be understood to be the source of something as raw, if indispensable, as the demand for justice? For if that were the case, would not this new transcendent demand for justice make it inevitable?

Such questions do not constitute an argument. Rather, they are ontological probes into the nature of holiness. They seek to discern how the holy is related to what it means to be human. Justice now comes to be seen as the basic connection between the holy and the human. Justice is believed to be immediately accessible in human corporate self-awareness for, as Genesis puts it, humanity is made in the image of the God who is its creator. It is remarkable that this distinctive experience of divine justice in terms of a particular narrative has as its corollary that it not exhausted by its historical context. It is to be available for this people in the unknown future and for all people as well. Did not the one God make all people in his image?

Holiness can be understood in many ways. In the biblical tradition, it bears repeating, its foundational meaning was rooted in a decisive event of liberation. Release from bondage issued in an enduring connection (covenant) between the liberated and the holy. This connection led to a second bonding: justice is both an entitlement and a demand: You who expect justice must give it. But also, in this same tradition, this double understanding of justice was often challenged and frequently compromised. For example:

- *Subsequent to the exodus narrative, justice was commonly, even canonically, recruited to justify war fighting. It goes something like this: "What's the point of freedom if you don't have real estate? Kill whomever has not known your liberation, whomever stands in your way. Freedom and justice are not intended for everyone—only for you and yours." So, it turns out, they are not really holy after all. Their usefulness is merely rhetorical.*
- *Worship understood as the dramatic enactment of the connection between transcendent holiness and the human need for justice proved fragile. Primordial patterns of sacrifice surfaced seeking to placate the holy now commonly seen as an insatiable recipient of sacrifice rather than the initiator, the well-spring, of justice. The holy increasingly came to be seen as passive. The holy became a reactor desiring to be served rather than the active actor demanding the community as a whole to be just. Transcendence as passivity, it was believed, could be managed by systems of sacrifice of placation. The Bible gives major canonical attention to the conflict between these two positions. The literary tradition beginning with Amos cries out in protest against this cultic betrayal of transcendent justice. Sufficient to say, Amos was not well received.*

So what does this prophetic tradition (Moses to Jesus), have to do with what is real? In a vast variety of contexts, prophets consistently insisted that transcendence cannot be banished from time and space, The holy will come and is coming upon us here and now. Isaiah of Jerusalem reports hearing an angel in the Temple chanting that both "heaven and earth are full of the glory of God." [4] Every day, still today, this line is a part of the most commonly used hymn in the worship of the church everywhere (Orthodox, Roman Catholic, and Protestant). The oldest Gospel says that this vision of the holy in time and space was the theme of Jesus' first sermon. Right here in little Nazareth far indeed from Jerusalem, the reign of God is breaking in among us now. [5] Here? Now?

How can this be? The moment we call "now" is immediately past, not now any more. So where is the holy? World religions offer different answers. Again, the Hebrew tradition is distinctive. It counsels: Do not despair that you cannot fly to some other world. Do not seek a timeless, spaceless realm where transcendence and nothing else (or, in some versions, only nothingness) prevail. Transcendence happens in, with, and under all that is in the present world. The infinite is within the finite. The Holy is an event of enduring creativity, healing, and love in a perishing world. This is the reality that evokes the faith that makes justice and freedom both possible and necessary. This is the holiness that cannot be escaped.

In the first century there first appeared a collection of portraits of what holiness looks like in practice. Over time and across cultures that small stream became a mighty, incomparable flood with no sight of abatement. Probably the best way to begin exploring these human signs of transcendence-in-space-and-time is to look at the oldest of them. Even a brief overview, noting their differences and continuities, can help us see how a search for transcendent justice and freedom is really possible.

The focus of the signs was a man called Joshua, whom the world today knows as Jesus of Nazareth and whose first disciples called Lord and Messiah. The most significant of these texts, in chronological order, are: [6]

**1. Paul's picture of Jesus as the Messiah crucified and risen for Israel and for all humankind.** Paul sketched it in at least seven surviving letters beginning with I Thessalonians probably in the year 41 and ending with Romans in 56.

**2. Mark's picture of Jesus as the action, suffering, and mystery of the Son of Man** was probably written in the late 60's or early 70s.

**3. Matthew's picture of Jesus as the new Moses in blocks of narrative and reflection** was probably written between 80 and 90.

**4. Luke's picture of Jesus as the Savior of Israel and therefore of all nations** was probably written around 85, or possibly anywhere from 75 to 95.

**5. John's picture of Jesus as God's insertion of light, life, and love into a hostile world. This Gospel is a community effort which was slowly formed over a period of forty-five years: Phase one: mid 50s to late 80s; phase two: ca. 90; phase three: ca. 100; phase four: 100-110.**

The five pictures are a gallery in which color, shape, and perspective differ markedly. The pictures are voices from different times and places and seem determined not to sing in unison. They are rather, a polyphonic chorus unafraid of dissonance, suspense, and outburst of creative energy. Each picture reflects something of Jesus and something of the writer's own faith in him as the supreme agent of God's mercy, justice and freedom. Over time, and even over the globe, each document has demonstrated a kind of sacramental capacity to evoke faith in Jesus as well. What did Paul and the writers of the Gospels see? The sequence and contexts of their writing influence their content.

### (1) What did Paul see?

Paul was first up to bat. What could be difficult—commending a Jewish Messiah to various non Jews, a "king" whose life ended with his being killed by a group of important political and religious authorities? They had agreed at least once: this man must be eliminated. Ever since the crucifixion of Jesus various theories have been offered to explain why it happened, even why it had to happen. Images have been drawn from liturgies of sacrifice, from law courts demanding punishment, from battlefields and athletic contests. None is useless. None is fully adequate. The best may be the oldest, the one proposed at the end of Genesis. Joseph forgave his murderous brothers by saying, "Even though you intended to do harm, God intended it for good." [7]

How can good come from evil? Justice from injustice? Freedom from bondage? Life from death? Resurrection from crucifixion?

The last of these is based on the rumor that Paul, a one-time persecutor of Jesus' followers, had heard. That report, by itself, had not been convincing. By his own admission it would take an overwhelming vision of holiness as God's Yes to a crucified Messiah to fuel his own spiritual revolution. He was not converted to a different religion. He repeatedly insisted that it was the discovery of a much deeper, much broader, meaning in Israel's ancient covenants that had transformed him. A new world had appeared on the horizon. In spite of formidable enemies, the crucified prophet from Nazareth was God's agent, a new kind of Messiah who lives to bring God's justice and love to all humankind. The ancient covenants had been expanded by a new reality, the resurrection of Jesus. The holy had newly appeared as a universal bestowal of God's own justice and freedom. The catalyst was not an invention of Paul. It was the witness he had first rejected, the personal discovery that holiness has trumped death. It always will.

The theological problem is not how could a tentmaker have had a vision of the holy. Visions are not unusual. The issue is how can a crucified criminal be Israel's messiah. Where's the justice in that? Justice, of course, had been understood as the obligation for obedience to the law understood as the law of love. But now an event has compelled a deep reinterpretation of the justice of God. When a godly life is rewarded by being tortured as a criminal, then justice as a reward for goodness has been exposed as a failure. But when God embraces this chosen one as his word-event (*dabar*) of a justice now seen as reconciliation, mercy, and endless life, a new kind of justice has been born. This justice is not an exhortation to the pious nor a judgment on sinners. The news is that humankind has been redefined by someone's actually living a godly life. What an outrage! That life was clearly a judgment on universal wickedness. But it is mostly God's own new creation, a display of God's participation in the griefs and sorrows of his creation now fully demonstrated in his healing presence in the life, death, and resurrection of Jesus.

Since Jesus had insisted that God's holiness is fundamentally God's love, then that holiness cannot be a threat but is an embrace, especially an embrace of people burdened by an awareness of their own moral failure. God's holiness is also needed to override the human sense of moral failure. Paul came to see it in a kind of parable, based no doubt on his own experience in court rooms. He showed how a judge can declare the accused "not guilty" regardless of whether the accused feel or do not feel they are guilty. In this scenario it is the judge who decides, not the accused. So, then, for people of faith, the holy can be pictured as a judge who has the capacity to declare the accused to be accepted as just. This justification is not a human moral achievement. It is a demonstration of how the holy can prevent human moral failure from overpowering the basic design, the intent, of God.

That everyone is a sinner in one way or another there can be no doubt—especially when humanity is rightly understood to have both social and personal dimensions. Justification of sinners by a gracious God and received by faith, Paul's formulation, evokes little interest from the morally casual who, as the saying goes, couldn't care less about their moral behavior. Justification of sinners is more a problem for the self-righteous, the self-justifiers, who are confident of their own moral superiority. "Surely God," they believe, "is obligated to reward the morally excellent (like me) and punish the reprobates–like a lot of people I could name. Who needs to be justified by faith when one's own record has been so outstanding? Looking back, I have no regrets."

Maybe Paul's insight into the moral depth of God's justification of the unjust can only be heard by a minority. That does not make it trivial. After all, not everyone is morally casual, proud of their cleverness in being able to avoid virtue and its problems. Humble people do exist, quite aware of their own shortcomings and the serious moral failures of their communities. Are these people doomed then to feel perpetually guilty? That would be dismissive of Jesus' achievement. Moral assurance can be a do-it-yourself project but with predictably dismal results. But it can also be a gift, a bestowal from another. Paul identifies Jesus as God's agent to bring that gift. Jesus is that gift. We are told he took special delight in eating and drinking with all sorts of sinners and outsiders. Actually, if you don't see yourself as a sinner, you probably won't feel that you fit in with that bunch.

Faith, thus, is not a doctrine nor a moral achievement. Faith is the holy at work within us, fully accepting us-- just as flawed as we suspect we really are. This acceptance is the work of justice actively healing a seriously sick humanity. Holy justice is not an abstract remote coldness, imperiously distant. The holy can now be seen as having reconstituted justice to become a gift to all who are open to receive it.

This is not the end of the matter. All this is but a foretaste of what is to come: The whole creation is destined to be set free from its bondage to death. It is destined to share in the glory of the freedom of the children of God.[8] Paul has a cosmic vision: Israel's glory in Jesus is actually an earnest for the whole creation.

## (2) What did Mark see?

About fourteen years after Paul had explored the implications of what the Messiah had achieved, a Greek-speaking Christian, possibly a disciple of Peter in Rome, brilliantly created a new literary genre, not quite a biography in the modern sense, but a brief, selective summary of key events in the life of Jesus. We call this little book the Gospel of Mark. Then, about fifteen years after that, two other Gospels appeared both based on Mark's. One was named in honor of a disciple of Jesus and the other for a Gentile companion of Paul. [9] These three Gospels of Mark, Matthew, and Luke, form a literary triptych. They clearly have the same subject: Messiah Jesus, but it is just as clear that they do their work in quite different ways. Some readers find this three-fold diversity an embarrassment. Some find it a creative achievement. And some don't even notice it.

Modern readers are usually surprised to see that half of Mark's narrative deals with just a few days at the end of Jesus' life. The first half is a hurried overview of his ministry in Galilee. The focus is first on John, the Baptizer, then on controversies in Galilee followed by a selection of miracle stories and the selection and training of disciples. The second half begins with this Gospel's dramatic pivot, Peter's clumsy confession that Jesus is Messiah and is followed by a vision connecting Jesus with key Old Testament leaders. The action then slows down: three predictions of the coming passion, a ministry in Jerusalem, warnings about the end time, and finally, deliberate emphasis on the Holy Week. The Easter account is abrupt.

What is the point of the oldest Gospel? It stresses Daniel's expectation that at the end-time "one like a son of man" (a human figure) will come from heaven (God pictured as an "Ancient One") to receive "dominion and glory and kingship . . . that all peoples should serve him." [8] Mark indicates that Jesus freely used this title to identify himself although the disciples apparently did not do so. In Mark, "Son of Man" is used to refer to a kingship displayed (a) in a life of healing and witness and (b) in a death marked by humiliation, betrayal, and rejection. "Son of Man" had referenced the coming of an apocalyptic catastrophe. Could Mark have made it any clearer that Jesus understood his own ministry of witness, healing and suffering as the demonstration of the end-time? Mark's preoccupation with the passion of Jesus as catastrophic is testimony to its importance of the apparent failure of his mission. How could a kingship which ends with the public execution of its king not be a catastrophe?

But Mark does not settle for the obvious. He seems reluctant to state simply just what his point really is. Instead, as it now stands, Mark seems to end on an unresolved chord; its original ending may have been lost. What is certain though is this: a catastrophe for traditional religion and culture is, for God, a break-through to an unimaginable victory. On the cross Jesus was heard to pray the psalm that begins "My God, my God, why have you forsaken me?" It is impossible that he did not know that this psalm had as its climax: "You have rescued me (O Lord), I will tell of your name to my brothers and sisters in the midst of the great congregation." [10] Mark's account of the rejection of the Son of Man and his kingship, which he so vividly underscores, ironically demonstrates the power of the Ancient One to achieve divine purposes in spite of human wickedness. The crucifixion of the Son of Man is not a defeat. It is the way the Ancient One, not subdued by catastrophe, uses it for a decisive achievement.

### (3) What did Matthew see?

The author of the Gospel of Matthew, deeply conservative in many ways, saw that the Gospel of Mark was a definitive model for any effort to describe the significance of the crucified Son of Man. But it was also incomplete on at least two levels. (a) Mark largely neglects to supply the content of Jesus' teaching. Probably the memory of what he had said was well known in oral form among his followers. But someone has to scoop up, protect, and enhance the tradition. (b) The rapidly growing community of Jewish Christians needed what Mark had neglected: materials demonstrating the deeply Jewish character of Jesus mission and message. Even casual readers may note how similar these two Gospels are in structure. But if they are not familiar with the Hebrew Scriptures, they many not notice the major role they play in shaping Matthew's Gospel.

The Torah (traditionally known as the Five Books of Moses) describes the origins of Israel in terms of the background, content, and significance of the exodus. Matthew takes five great heaps of teaching material to fill out Mark's Gospel. Structural parallels connecting Jesus to Moses imply that they are both prophetic teachers commissioned to lead a new people. [11] The new Moses affirms and surpasses the old in many ways. He is an embodiment of the central meaning of the Torah by actually demonstrating what it means to love God above all things and to love one's neighbor as oneself. That is why he is a compassionate healer, a host for hungry multitudes and even a master of the waters. He leads a new community out of servitude, a community which is open to all. As a messianic king he surpasses violent, adulterous David. He captures Daniel's vision of the Son of Man coming at the end time to be judge of all. Above all he heralds the coming of God's new reign for all, a reign that boldly dares send eleven surviving disciples to leave everything to go out to make disciples of all nations.

But Matthew can also be a troubling text. Modern readers have complained that he is excessively critical of the Jewish religious leaders of the first century. According to Raymond E. Brown, however, Matthew's portrayals of the scribes and Pharisees are criticisms "not untypical of the harsh criticism of one Jewish group by another Jewish group" at that time. [12] Matthew was a Jewish writer addressing a Jewish community. Generally speaking, the severest criticism rises within a particular religious community, not between different religious communities. That certainly has been true for Judaism, Christianity, and Islam. More significant is Brown's associated observation: "The casuistic approach to law criticized by Matthew is inevitable in any established religion, including the Church…(Those today) studying Matthew might profitably go through chapter 23 seeking parallels in Christianity and/or society for the condemned behavior." No single religious tradition can claim to have been innocent of hypocrisy–as its most devout followers have not been reluctant to point out.

### (4) What did Luke see?

The authors of the Gospels of Matthew and Luke probably did not know of each other's work but shared a common enthusiasm for the multifaceted message and dramatic structure of Mark as well as a recognition that the church in which they lived in the last decade of the first century had come to need a larger

Gospel, one which could include teaching material still available in the oral tradition but not used by Mark. They were writing for different communities with different concerns and thus produced distinctive narratives. Their expansions of Mark give the reader a richer record than either alone could provide. While Matthew had focused on Jesus' rootedness in the history of Israel, Luke, probably a Gentile convert to Judaism, gave that less emphasis. His distinctive interest is the radically inclusive significance of the good news of Jesus. He is God's messiah who connects Israel to universal history. His two volume project has three foci: *Israel* (as represented in the Hebrew Scriptures), *Jesus* (Luke's Gospel) and the *Church* sent in mission to the whole world (The Acts.) Jesus is the event that makes these connections possible.

The global reach of the good news is not only a matter of ancient history and current events; it is immediately inclusive of present culture in Luke's time. Attention is given to Mary, the mother of Jesus. What would Christmas look like without Luke's stories and songs about the annunciation and the nativity? Women continue to appear frequently: We read of a destitute yet generous widow and of another poor woman who had lost her money. And there is a persistent widow who overpowers a grumpy judge. There are accounts of Jesus caring for a hemorrhaging woman, a risky Sabbath-day healing of a crippled woman, and the raising of the widow's son at Nain. Women are not just recipients of his attention. They act freely. We read of a sinful woman who shocked the disciples by bathing Jesus' feet with her tears, kissing and anointing them with oil. The hospitality shown the strange Galilean rabbi by Mary and Martha at their home east of Jerusalem is surprising. How could they have known to trust him? On Easter morning it was a mostly unnamed group of Galilean women who had walked with Jesus all the way to Jerusalem who were the first to hear that the Son of Man had been raised from the dead. Perhaps they were a part of the body of women activists who had been supporting Jesus and the disciples financially all along.. Think of the people who would have been shocked by all this.

Not only women but children are in the spotlight: Children are set forth as role models for adults. That could be dangerous. But it could also help grown-ups find their way back to God if they dared try. And only Luke remembers that when Jesus himself was a child he knew already then that he had more than one father. Doesn't everyone know that?

Another surprise: Samaritans are conventionally distained in Judea and Galilee. Luke pictures the disciples urging Jesus to get "fire from heaven" so they can kill them off. Jesus responds by rebuking not the Samaritans, but the disciples. On another occasion he presses the issue by making up a story which features a Samaritan as the hero, an exemplar for his morally challenged disciples.

Other strange protagonists pop up: It is not an obviously virtuous son, but his brother who had wasted his inheritance in dissolute living who is a moral hero. A dishonest estate manager who cooks the books for his own gain has something to teach the disciples about virtue.

How did all this go over? Luke says that Jesus was aware that his behavior had earned him a dubious reputation. He once observed:

*John the Baptist came in the strictest austerity and you say he is crazy. Then the Son of Man came, enjoying life, and you say, 'Look, a drunkard and a glutton, a bosom-friend of the tax-collector and the outcasts!' Ah well, the children of wisdom know what wisdom really is.* [14] *(7:33ff.)*

In sum, Luke's two volume opus begins at Jerusalem's Bethlehem suburb with two marvelous narratives. It ends at Rome, the capital of the Empire, with Paul in prison welcoming all who came to him by proclaiming the coming of the reign of God right under the emperor's nose: From Jerusalem to Rome: Luke has given us an account of a fateful meeting of two very different worlds. He has given us something new: a geography of salvation.

### (5) What did John see?

Just how did it come to pass that the Gospel usually judged the most theological of the four turns out to be the one most favored by crowds hoisting **3:16** signs at football games? How did it come to pass that the Gospel most favored devotionally by lay people is the one that intellectuals find the most controversial? Perhaps it is no accident that this Gospel which evokes such a wide a range of responses is particularly invested in the language of irony. How else could the vital positive tension between the divine and the human be signaled and sustained?

This Gospel shows how God has done something decisively new by freely entering into creation through the life of the Son of Man. For God, life in the flesh is no problem because creation in the form of a human life is capable of bearing the fullness of God's glory. The Son of Man is God's creative word, the communication of God's presence in the flesh, a flesh suddenly full of God's own healing grace and life giving truth. There is no need to be anxious about the end of the world, for the day of judgment has now come in the life and death of Jesus. There is no more need to fear or cause others to fear death, for the Son of Man is the resurrection and the life who has made it possible for those connected to him to live for a future radiant with unimaginably abundant life. The crucifixion was intended to be a mock coronation. But the mockery is mocked by God. Its intent has been subverted. Water can become delicious wine. A ghastly Roman cross can become a conduit for glory.

In the vast sea of academic research, the stream associated with such names as C. H. Dodd and Raymond E. Brown has provided a way for approaching the Gospel and Epistles of John that has proved not only critical, but constructive and coherent. [15] Brown theorizes that the Gospel of John was the work of a Johannine community at work from the mid 50s to as late as 110. Three stages of development can be identified:

*(a) Presumably Mark and the other sources used by Matthew and Luke did not include everything the early oral tradition had contained. Among other memories of Jesus some had been especially significant for the intimate, unnamed person the Gospel highlights simply as "the disciple whom Jesus loved."*

*(b) These memories were treasured in a distinctive community which preserved and expanded them in the light of their spiritual*

*experience in the last decade of the first century in Ephesus (west Turkey) or Syria.*

*(c) The final collector of these traditions was an evangelist at the beginning of the second century who, with significant creative skill, shaped them to complete the fourth Gospel.*

The Johannine tradition provides a distinctive witness to Jesus similar to and different from that provided by Mark-Matthew-Luke. Careful readers can easily note the unique character of its message. The structure of John's Gospel in its final form is also unique. Unlike the other Gospels, it provides a prologue about creation and an epilogue noting the destiny of the beloved disciple. Within this frame, the Gospel presents two bodies of material:

*(a) In "The Book of Signs," Jesus reveals God in a series of serious/humorous dialogues exploring misunderstandings and a limited number of miracles but including three not mentioned in the other Gospels. The writer is particularly interested in Jewish liturgical life as celebrated in four religious festivals. The signs are direct challenges which evoke both belief and rejection.*

*(b) In "The Book of Glory," Jesus returns to the Father in his death and resurrection/ascension. He bestows the Spirit of life, abundant and eternal, upon those who believe in him and his mission.*

The community of John saw something extraordinary. Questions galore sweep over the Gospel's readers: "Was it really necessary, or even wise, to paint a picture so different from that which we find in Mark-Matthew-Luke? Or does the ongoing life of the Spirit in the community make John's witness necessary? Is it really possible to see that the catastrophe of Jesus' crucifixion could be used by love to manifest the glory of God? Can mere "belief" be an adequate word for being able to abide in God, to participate in the revelation of the Father through the Son in the Spirit? Do these kinds of differences among the Gospels enrich or hamper the witness of the community today? What questions do you want to add? What do these five pictures of the Messiah have to do with faith?

Our quick overview of these five first century pictures certainly seems far removed from a lot of contemporary religion—conservative or liberal. For that matter, the pictures do not seem to fit each other very well either, perhaps because they were intended for quite different communities which did not have the same concerns. For that matter, do they really connect with any of the child's experience of faith discussed in the first chapter? The lack of simplicity is not the problem. A child may think of faith in many ways too. Faith is an adventure, faith is not being afraid, faith is being and staying connected, faith means asking questions.

The temptation that tidy minds may find irresistible is to try to edit the five pictures of Jesus so they will conform to one's own personal life experience. The pictures were intended, however, to challenge and transform human experience, not to conform to it. Falling into that temptation at this point would be premature and would short circuit our project. Each of the pictures–not only John's–was developed in a community engaged in worship, witness, and acts of service. Human communities are internally diverse–always. So it would be impossible to determine precisely what everyone in each of the five picture-making communities meant by faith. That was not their problem. It is ours, however, and needs to be addressed. But not quite yet.

## CHAPTER THREE

### *What Does God Have to Do With It?*

Of course God has everything to do with faith, with belief. So runs the conventional assumption. But how about people who do not believe in God or at least do not believe in the way the word "God" has been presented to them? It would not be right to say they have no faith, no beliefs at all. Many of them would say they are not religious because they are committed to what they understand to be the truth and that religion does not measure up to that. They are not saying that they have no commitments. Some would say that because of their commitment to the truth, they cannot believe in the God that has been presented to them. Then there are those much larger groups of people who sometimes believe and sometimes do not believe, who move between some conventional understandings of religion and various sentiments of agnosticism.

None of this is very surprising. It is common in the modern world. What is not so well known is that in the West, at the beginning of the modern era when late medieval religion was coming under very serious criticism, early Protestantism began to sense problems with the traditional proofs for the existence of God. Well before Immanuel Kant showed the fallacies in the traditional proofs, Reformation theologians began to explore strategies which would make such proofs not only irrelevant, but irreverent.

Believers had seen that the God whom the philosophers had claimed they had proved to exist was markedly different from the God of Abraham, Isaac and Jacob. Would this God then be "more real" than the God of the Bible? Or were they identical? How could that be proved? Is the notion that human beings have the power to transcend God by making God the object of their thinking not impious? Holiness is what transcends us, not something which we might capture if we were clever enough.

There is a second problem here as well. Why should they who live in a loving relationship have to suspend loving until they can prove to a third party that something called love actually exists? What would be a proof sufficiently strong to convince that third party–who may never have known what it is to be loved–to be able to say "Oh, yes, now I know that love really does exist?"

It was not just mystics who had found philosophical proofs for God's existence to be irrelevant for the religious life. Some monastics began to discover that a deliberate "turn to the subject" could actually be a major resource–rather than being dismissed as an unfortunate weakness. Growing skepticism about the validity of the old scholasticism was stimulated by related movements in Europe. Renaissance scholarship in Italy had been championing the need to recover "the original sources" of Western culture. Theologians began to follow that lead. For them a return to the sources meant chiefly a recovering of the biblical witness as preserved in its original languages, Hebrew and Greek. "We know what the Church is saying. But what did the prophets and apostles say?" Humanism emerged as a way to leap over medieval debris. It did not see itself hostile to Christianity.

One of its earliest of these more adventuresome academics, a professor of Old Testament literature, quickly discovered that his texts had a great deal to say about the problem of gaining access to the reality of God. Moreover, he saw that his sources could have immediate impact on religious life outside the classroom. What does it mean when Moses says to Israel, "You are to have no other gods?" This is a rejection of polytheism, of course, but it is more than that. There was no general public worship of "other gods" in medieval Christendom. Does that make the Hebrew commandment obsolete? Or can they speak to confused Christians in sixteenth century Saxony? The professor was a Catholic priest who had been assigned to preach regularly at Saint Mary's Church in Wittenberg. His sermons dealing with the Ten Commandments had attempted to explore a present-day meaning for "You are to have no other gods." That had gone well. Well then, why not rework this material for use as the content of a teacher's manual for other clergy? They too need to rethink what it means for congregations to be told "You are to have no other gods." Here is his decidedly non-scholastic response:

*A "god" is the term for that to which we are to look for all good and in which we are to find refuge in all need. Therefore, to have a god is nothing else than to trust and believe in that one with your whole heart. As I have often said, it is the trust and faith of the heart alone that make both God and an idol. If your faith and trust are right, then your God is the true one. Conversely, where your trust is false and wrong, there you do not have the true God. For these two belong together, faith and God. Anything on which your heart relies and depends, I say, that is really your God.* [1]

His reflection is, of course, circular. His description of the inseparability of faith and God is not an argument. It is not the proof of the existence of faith or of God. It is a recognition of an inescapable characteristic of all human experience. It is an observation, easily replicated, that we humans are defined by our relationships.

Scholastic theology, Roman Catholic and Protestant, did not buy in on this notion of an inseparable connection between faith and God. Faith continued to be understood as a giving of assent to propositions about God—not as a risky act of trusting in an other (whom you do not control) with your whole heart. The Church's Reformation understanding of faith as different from an act of the mind or will did win wide acceptance. But once it received canonical status in the foundational literature of the Protestant movement, it might be ignored but could not be forgotten. In the nineteenth century, Brother Martin's insight was revived by his distant sons, Sören Kierkegaard and Friedrich Nietzsche—albeit for dramatically different reasons.

In the twenty-first century, thinking of faith and the holy as inseparably united could prove quite useful. For one thing, it immediately breaks down the barrier that separates believers from non-believers. From this perspective, there are no non-believers. We all are believers, atheists and theists alike. We just don't agree on what it is we believe in. That is no surprise. Atheists don't all agree among themselves and theists don't either.

All of us are stuck with the same problem: We are all believers in something or another. No one can prove philosophically, mathematically, scientifically, psychologically or in any other way that one's beliefs do not rest on unproven assumptions. A particularly brilliant demonstration of this apparently distressing news was offered by the Czech mathematician, Kurt Goedel, who proved that every mathematical system rests on assumptions that the system accepts but cannot prove. [2]

Atheists and agnostics do not merely reject what they believe to be traditional religious statements. They are more positive; they are engaged in a search for the truth. It would not be wrong to say that functionally their God is that truth which has the power to expose falsehood. Theirs is a noble effort. But what, we all end up having to ask, is truth? Is it only a conventional term for a current consensus? Or was Plato right: truth is an essential and universal presupposition to which all thinkers appeal in every rational struggle? Or was Pilate right in using philosophical skepticism as a cover for moral cowardice? Is there a fourth possibility? How do you prove whichever you chose that your position is true? If your actionable God--regardless of whatever your religious/non religious brand may be—is that which you base your life on, then you are a believer. You really do believe in something.

That may be less than reassuring. It could seem that now there is an astronomical number of gods. The undetermined number of gods each confused person has times the number of people who have ever lived or will live would have to be incomprehensibly large. Given all the theoretically possible options, it is remarkable how relatively few have surfaced.

When we shift to the traditional religious uses of the word "god," it is striking how important monotheism has been for religious communities in the West and, in some ways, in the East as well. But even that doesn't get us very far. A big problem in efforts at interreligious dialogue lies in determining whether different religions can recognize each other's claim to be monotheistic. Technically, the Israelites before the eighth century prophets were henotheists rather than monotheists. It's likely that in large measure this is still true for most people in the Abrahamic tradition today: Jewish, Christian, and Muslim. Henotheists claim they worship one not many gods. But they assume, or sometimes insist, that people of other religions do not worship the same God that they do. If all the daughters and sons of Abraham were monotheists in fact, and not just in rhetoric, then they would as a matter of faith have to insist *gladly* that they and all other monotheists are one since all worship the one and only God. The Hebrew, Greek, and Arabic languages use different words to name this Holy One. But if Christians do not believe they worship *Allah*, and Jews *Theos*, and Muslims *Elohim*, then are they not henotheists rather than monotheists? They behave as though they believe, "Your god is not my God." Interfaith discussions commonly fail to identify what God's role is in what the participants have in common. It is true that many of the differences among Jews, Christians, and Muslims are precious for each and thus apparently insurmountable.

What is resisted, however, and potentially far more significant, is that in each of these cases, their belief in the reality of the one God carries with it the responsibility to acknowledge related convictions of deepest import. In each of these traditions the one God is consistently recognized as a God of compassion and justice, as acting in history to reveal a divine purpose, and as the ultimate Creator of all that is. These basic affirmations saturate the Hebrew Scriptures, the New Testament and the Koran. None of these sacred texts attempts to provide a logical structure designed to show how these three different convictions coincide. In each tradition God is the Almighty Creator who reveals his redemptive purpose in a historically unique, unrepeatable situation. These two convictions are deeply connected to a third. In each tradition there is a special people who are recipients of this wonderful revelation and who are charged to live faithfully in it. The following chart may help understand this morphology of faith. It indicates that in three different cultural periods, belief in one God carried two consequences: belief in the decisive character of an historical event clusters as revelatory and belief in the trustworthiness of a community of faith to receive and transmit this wonder. The linguistic terms differ, of course; the shape of experience is identical. If there is no sacred community, there is no way for the revelation to be known. If there is no holy One, there is no encounter with transcendent holiness. If there is no content to the holiness revealed, the community can not exist.

| **HOLY TRIAD** | | |
|---|---|---|
| GOD → | REVELATION | → COMMUNITY |
| GOD ← | REVELATION | ← COMMUNITY |
| *Elohim* | Torah | Israel |
| *Theos* | Messiah | Church |
| *Allah* | Koran | Islam |

Each of the three traditions has been shaped historically to describe the relationships among its three elements, that is why each does it in a different way. None of the traditions can tolerate the omission of any of its own three elements. All see that unity is not undifferentiated sameness. Unity comprehends distinctions; it does not abolish them. Unity is socially dynamic, not a non-historical abstraction like a number, for example. Unity is disclosed in historical time and space. One does not have to go to an ideal world to find it. It is an event in this world.

Why did this Abrahamic legacy develop differently among the three traditions? It is not because Judaism and Islam are truly monotheistic while Christianity is a disguised form of polytheism. A calmer assessment is possible. The Christian movement was confident that it had been given the gift of wisdom as a part of the gift of faith. The Greek Church, in particular, was eager to worship the holy as the wisdom which gives insight for gaining access to the divine life. That conviction was based on the insistence that the holy can be both mystery and knowable. The two are inseparably connected. Mystery leads to knowledge; knowledge leads back to mystery.

A people whose ancestors could build the Parthenon, that architectural wedding of geometry and high art, had strong reason to believe that they could celebrate an incomparably greater union—the connection between what God had done in Christ through the Spirit and their own God-given capacity to speak of this faithfully. The confidence that this could actually be done appears to have been more robust in the third century than it is in the twenty-first. What we tend to see as a problem they saw as an achievement.

Early Christianity understood itself as an Abrahamic tradition that experienced both hostility (persecution) and opportunity (mission) in the Roman Empire. Opportunity would require embracing as well as critiquing their culture's intellectual heritage. Negatively: how could it be possible for the theologians not to notice that they were thinking in Greek and Latin? Why should it be required of them as Greeks to have to say "no" to their cultural identity in order to say "yes" to the good news of Jesus? He had come not to destroy but to save. Positively: Why should not the Greek confidence in the power of *logos*, the operation of reason in both mind and matter, be seen as a part of the revelation of the divine, a local name for the wisdom of God? The question quickly became an affirmation of enormous potentiality.

Today the issue is framed differently. We have options. We need to ask (1), whether the design that formed the doctrine of the Holy Trinity was suitably attentive to the actions and promise of the holy in Israel and among the Gentiles? Or (2), should we ignore history and settle for understanding the holy as a sublime impersonal abstraction? Or (3), should we ignore history in another way by attempting to picture the holy as a solitary, sovereign tribal monarch incapable of change? The twenty-first century's revival of interest in rethinking the doctrine of the Trinity would certainly have surprised—and probably displeased—the theologians, left and right, of the early twentieth century. The latter presumed that the historical forms of their theology should be regarded as eternal as God. The former assumed that wisdom means only learning how to get religion to accommodate itself to the alarming zeitgeist of modern Europe.

Regardless of our response, religion itself keeps right on chugging along. Does anyone seriously think that the Abrahamic tradition is about to expire? If not, what happens when their theologians bestir themselves to enter into an inter-faith dialogue?

All three Abrahamic faiths believe that one God has been revealed in particular times and places to a particular people. In some ways they share a common legacy. The Hebrew Bible is a major portion of the Christian Bible and is prominent in Christian preaching and liturgies. Islam honors Jesus, his ascension and his blessed mother. On the other hand, Judaism and Islam do agree at one central point: revelation is basically an ancient text, Torah or Koran. Some Christians have sought to agree by including their Bible in this consensus. This strategy results, however, in Christians' having two somewhat contradictory foci of revelation, a person and a book. Furthermore, this approach actually repudiates a central theme of Jesus' teaching, confuses the consistent witness of the New Testament, is alien to Christianity's historic creeds and confessions, and shows itself to be theologically incoherent.[3] Thus a central interfaith problem remains: Where is the holy decisively revealed? In a book and if so, which one? In a human life and if so, whose?

So the consensus among the three traditions turns out to be only partial, not comprehensive. Exploring the inestimable value of that incomplete consensus is the task which the three faith communities have barely begun. Their reluctance to make a move suggests that they have not been deeply attentive to the legacy of Abraham of Iraq who understood faith to mean trusting God as his friend by moving with him into an unknown future. Learning to recognize the triadic character of each of the tradition's fundamental beliefs could help all of them come to a deeper, more mature, appreciation of their familial connections. The way forward cannot be reductionistic: "What do we have to give up?" It is a challenge: "How can we be faithful to the God that Abraham knew as we move ahead into an unknown future? How can we even begin to do that if we do not learn to listen to our Abrahamic sisters and brothers?"

In such a conversation it would be necessary to consider what each member of the family understands by the words "God," "revelation" and "community." Are they inseparable? How are they distinctive? What are the perceived strengths and weaknesses in that non-biblical name, "Trinity?" Here, for example, is how a Christian approach could be framed:

- *Each of the traditions deals with the same problem: How can the holy, the eternal, be understood to be present in historical time?*

- *The Trinity is the non-biblical word which many Christians use to respond to this question. It has nothing to do with arithmetic. It is a transformative way of speaking of the identity of the holy.* [4] *Three words can say this: "God is Love."* [5] *Augustine got the point. Love is a trinity (1) of action which presupposes the presence of (2) one who loves and (3) one who is beloved.* [6]

- *God is understood to be active in the cosmos and history as well as in the human capacity to participate consciously in both. That action is discernable in the struggles of creation, the struggles of history, the struggles of human self-awareness.* [7] *The three articles of the classic creeds briefly summarize the work of God in these very different theaters, i.e., the creation of all things, the crucifixion of the New Adam and the community of forgiven sinners.* [8]

- *Faith is the word we use for our human participation in God's struggles, confident that ultimately (and already in part) it is the love of God which shall prevail since love is stronger than death.* [9]

## CHAPTER FOUR

## *The First Gift*

Why is it embarrassing to say what it means to love--or to be loved?

We may even be afraid to try. We know no one expects us to do this perfectly. Of course not. But what should be infinitely harder would be attempting to say what it means to live in the infinite love of God. Yet here, oddly, we need not be afraid to try.

The basis for this strange state of affairs is still commonly, if not intellectually, acceptable. Children, if not always their parents, seem quite happy to sing Anna B. Warner's enduring, charming doggerel:

**Jesus loves me!
This I know
For the Bible tells me so.**

Children too young to read actually claim canonical support for their participation in divine love? Technically, they may be misquoting John 3:16, but that's not the point.

Knowing that one is loved is the point. Does not every child deeply need to know that? What happens when children sense, or are sure they know, that their parents do not love them with any consistency or even, alas, at all? Are those millions of children misled if they are encouraged to believe that love can be greater than anything their family could show them? Could the Bible's astonishing claim be really true?

It all depends. The Bible has often been called a love story. But that's a pretty sophisticated assessment, one which it is not likely that children would figure out for themselves. The claim would be false, and therefore unspeakably cruel, if there were no voice in the community who could show how it could be true. That voice could not be one of apathy or indifference, nor one of fanaticism or bigotry. It would have to be a voice informed by John's insight that "God is love, and those who abide in love, abide in God." [1] So where did John get that? In part from the community in which he abided. And in part as a post-resurrection, controversial breakthrough into a new understanding of the reality of God. That could work. All you need is a voice to show how the two Testaments could be read as a love story.

Of course, the voice would need to know that whatever else it may be, divine love is not mere eroticism nor easy sentimentality. In the biblical perspective, the voice would have understood that divine love has to do with multiple wonders: the primordial turning of chaos into goodness, the strange polarities of justice, and the ultimacy of interpersonal relationships. Here's one way to sketch it: Holy love is the sublime event which brings us all out of nothingness so we can live and move and have being. It is also the way holiness can transform us by the power of forgiveness. And it is that spirit that broods over everything, and feels like a warm wind lifting us mortal kites into eternal life.

So just how does the biblical saga, with all its turns and interruptions, turn out to be a coherent story about that divine love which excels all loves? We could make it difficult for ourselves if we were to begin where the Bible begins: with accounts of the creation. Few texts have proven more divisive than these—particularly in the modern era. There's not much love evident in all that controversy. But then does not great literature begin with confronting great problems? Let's go for it.

## In the Beginning

The traditional way to talk about God does that. Both the Torah and the Fourth Gospel begin with creation accounts. [2] But from the time of Marcion in the second century until well after Darwin in the nineteenth, the creation texts have been particularly controversial. The emergence of the natural sciences after the Enlightenment dramatically enlarged the scope of the problem. In the eighteenth century, biblical scholars made the problem even more difficult as they found previously neglected evidence of significant literary differences within the Bible itself. The contest among different understandings of the Bible was now found to be resident within the Bible.

In earlier times when most people were more apt to hear the Bible read than to read it themselves, the differences between Genesis' chapters one and two would not have been easy to notice. Later, as printing made Bibles generally accessible, a casual reader might have assumed that these two chapters describe a coherent sequence rather than a contrast in perspectives. Still later it became increasingly obvious--at least to a careful reader-- that these chapters employ different literary styles, use different vocabularies and present different understandings of God and creation. An influential theory proposed that Genesis 2:4b -3:24 was actually older than Genesis 1 :1-2:4a. It was labeled "J" by pioneering German Protestant scholars because of the document's use of the word "Jahwe" (or, as pronounced in English, "Yahweh") as the special name of Israel's God. Genesis 1:1-2:4 came to be labeled "P" because of evidence that it was the work of the Hebrew priestly community during or shortly after the Exile.

The discovery of the distinctiveness of the two traditions was mostly greeted with distain, if not alarm. Did not this research destroy the belief that the Bible was the word of God?

How could God have two different views of how the world was made? By the middle of the twentieth century, however, not only Protestant but Catholic and Jewish scholars had generally come to accept the validity of this pioneering work by Julius Wellhausen.

While today it has become a commonplace in academic communities, it is not well known among the general public.

Why should variety within the Bible seem a weakness? Do not the New Testament's four Gospels give a richer and truer understanding of how the Jesus movement arose and developed than any one Gospel could possibly do? Muslims, of course, would not agree. But why should not Christians? Have they not learned that *diatessarons* inevitably violate the integrity of sacred writings? Unfortunately, scholars and preachers have not been effective in generating appreciation for the literary and spiritual creativity of the Biblical writers. This is unfortunate. Why should we presume to prohibit the authors of the creation narratives to be permitted to be creative themselves? The priests who survived the Exile were not reluctant to attempt an up-date for the older J tradition. Nor did they suppress it. True conservatives, they liberally added their work to what they had received from the past—giving their new work, of course, primary seating in the house. As for the theological anxiety generated by the claim that the Bible had developed over time with each strata of its development actually capable of being dated, what is the problem with that? How could belief in a God who is active in history object to a revelation resident in a succession of historical memories?

Jewish creativity, of course, did not end with the writing of Genesis. The Gospel of John begins with a prologue that clearly honors Genesis 1: "In the beginning." It goes on to summarize, expand, and reformulate the priestly account, and so produces the Christian Bible's third major creation narrative. John's prologue has received enormous Christological and liturgical attention, but it has largely been ignored in theological reflection on the meaning of creation. Why this inattentiveness?

Even in a scientific age, these ancient Hebrew and Greek texts continue to fascinate readers. Their differences are unmistakable. Yet the later narratives presume the truth of their predecessors. It is richly ironic that these texts that so strikingly document the fact of change are commonly used to resist belief that religious understandings of creation can change.

Religious people have been said to have lost their religious faith because science, in particular arguments for evolution, has made the Bible incredible. It is increasingly clear that this tragic loss is not a problem which biology created but is rooted in an inadequate understanding of the Bible's formation. Reverence for this sacred library includes a respectful appreciation of how the Bible has evolved. Research has shown that the earliest strata of the Bible were not dismissed as obsolete by the later. All strata are still there. J lies under P which lies under John. What the community needed to know about creation was not terminated at one time in the past. The tradition itself, like the biblical boy who was thought by his parents to have been lost, has grown in size and wisdom and in favor with God and humankind.

## Creation Understood Creatively

A comparison of these three major accounts of creation in their order of authorship can be a revealing experience. The following grid highlights their particularities:

| TEXT | | |
|---|---|---|
| Genesis 2:4b-3:24 | Genesis 1:1-2:4a | John 1:1-18 |
| **DATE** | | |
| 10$^{th-9th}$ cent. BCE | 6$^{th}$ cent. BCE | 1$^{st}$ cent. CE |
| **CONTEXT** | | |
| Davidic Israel | Post-Exile Israel | Ephesus (Turkey) |
| **DIVINE NAME** | | |
| *Yahweh* | *Elohim* | *Theos/Logos* |
| **LITERARY NAME** | | |
| Yahwist narrative | Priestly liturgy | Johannine prologue |
| **LITERARY FORM** | | |
| Comic tragedy | Priestly redaction | Cosmological poem |
| **CORE MESSAGE** | | |
| Human choices and human sin | God's ordered and good universe | God communicates cosmos and history |

Take a closer look at the significance of these traditions. We begin with the oldest, the *Yahwist* account. Its primary focus is on humankind, i.e. in Hebrew, *Adam*, and his spouse, Eve. Some have suggested this text is the work of a woman: Notice Adam's absurd efforts to avoid responsibility by blaming others: the serpent (not an embodiment of evil but of craftiness), his wife, and finally, Yahweh. Perhaps avoiding responsibility is a major element in universal or original sin. The ancient Hebrews would not have missed the author's bold strokes of outrageous humor. Nor should we. For example:

- *A crafty snake persuades people to do what he wants— and they don't even seem to notice that it's odd that he can speak Hebrew.*
- *Adam and Eve invent loincloths made of leaves (ouch) so that who, exactly, won't see what?*
- *It's been a tough day; even Yahweh has to take a walk to cool off.*

The comedic style is not irreverent. It's used to highlight by bold contrast the author's major point, the history of unrighteousness. A fascinating little drama, seemingly naïve, introduces a history of human violence and consistent injustice. The Yahwist begins by enticing the reader to reflect seriously on an ugly theme: the history of tribal wickedness. This strategy works well. It encourages the listener to ask:

- *Is not every murder a fratricide?*
  *Originally we are only dirt? Is this then also our destiny?*
- *Why are people often discontented when they pause to reflect on the meaning of their lives? Have we lost a godly, splendid Eden somewhere along the way? Why do we mourn its apparent loss? Why expect anything other than the unsatisfactory world that we seem to be stuck with?*

- *Is not the Yahwist's dark view of human behavior echoed in every honest historian's chronicle—and in every evening's newscast? Why does it never go out of date?*

Creation for the *Yahwist* focuses on the creation of humankind, its choices and its moral incompetence. This is not really a naïve text. Its literary skill and intellectual insight catch the conscience of its readers since ancient times. Its antiquity does not obscure its truth. As for its humor, that evokes a bit of new irony. Atheists and Fundamentalists finally agree on at least one thing. Unlike the *Yahwist*, they seem to believe that religion teaches that the Fall in Eden happened once, not that it happens all the time.

Then there's the priestly account. However profound the *Yahwist* tradition may be, all that it represented, including its understanding of creation, met a fearful challenge during the Exile (587-538 BCE). The leaders of Judah were forced to emigrate eastward to Babylon, a strategy devised by the Babylonians to destroy utterly Israel's national identity. Israel's poets excel in telling of their shock, their dismay, at this catastrophe. Has the Lord abandoned Zion? What reader is not moved by the pathos of Psalms 74 and 137?

Surprisingly, however, the time of Exile in Babylon provided unanticipated opportunities. Encountering the much older Babylonian creation myth, "*Enuma elish*," (c. 1728-1686 BCE) for the first time must have been disturbing since its polytheism so radically contradicted their own *Yahwist* creation account. Many exiles must have rejected it outright. But others found a way to adapt it so that could enlarge, enrich and thus strengthen the Hebrew tradition. For example, "*Enuma elish*" spoke of a universe much larger than the earth assumed in the *Yahwist* tradition. The older myth had a cosmic sense which the *Yahwist* account lacked. Of course, the Babylonian scheme of a week of ten days would have to be modified to fit the restrictions of a six-day work week. But what would later prove profoundly significant is that unlike J, P understands humankind to succeed, not to precede, the creation of animals.

Most troubling, of course, was *"Enuma elish's"* polytheism. It regarded the sun and stars as gods—clearly an unacceptable notion for Israel. The myth's view of the creation as a conflict between the god Marduk and the dragon Tiamat was worse. That had to be changed. The priests did not see a need, however, to alter the belief that the planets are lanterns suspended on the underside of the great dome we call the sky, the dome that serves as a kind of reservoir that leaks water when it rains. Another problem: Small boys like to ask why the Bible says that there was light three days before the sun was made. And were birds really made before the fish? Where are the dinosaurs? And how could there be domestic cattle before people? The point, of course, is that the priests were liturgical poets and small boys usually are not.

The achievement of the priestly writers is brilliant. Their purpose was to respond to the splendor of the universe as they knew it, not by worshipping it in subservience, but by praising God as its creator. Of course they did their work many centuries before modern science emerged. Their task was to perform major surgery on pagan material so that it could serve their monotheistic faith. Had they, by some trick of literary magic, been able to produce a document that would conform to the standards of twenty-first century science, how could that have been conceivable to them or to anyone living after them until the twenty-first century? What they did do was what science can not do: produce a sacred document that boldly affirms a sublime creativity that infinitely transcends all that that human beings can control. The priestly creation account is not about gods in conflict. Rather, it sees creation as literally profane, i.e. not divine, not absolute, not self-made, not everlasting. Creation properly evokes awe and wonder and humility, not adoration nor subservience.

The story of creation can be read as a priestly liturgy: mysterious yet comprehensible at many levels, a display of power and beauty and goodness, a process partly understood by mortals and partly not. The poem's focus on what God's awful transcendence means for the faithful is echoed in its insistently repeated refrain: in all its parts the cosmos is good. Indeed, it is very good. To say that is a sheer act of faith, a belief with enormous practical consequences. It was never intended to be what today could be called a scientific analysis. To require that is to abuse it.

Of course Israel's reflections on creation are richer than two chapters in Genesis. Psalms, prophets, and wisdom texts celebrate the splendor of the natural world which, seen as a gift, evokes songs of grateful praise. Psalms 96-98 and 148 call on creation to declare God's glory to all humankind. Isaiah 40:12-31 sees the promised deliverance from exile as an act of God's transcendence over nature. Proverbs 8:22-31 holds that wisdom is God's agent in creation, his joyful companion from "before the beginning of the earth." Particularly remarkable are the Song of Solomon with its sustained celebration of human sexuality and Job 38-39 which sees nature as a challenge to religious unbelief not as its cause.

Later on, as Jewish writers began to write in Greek, someone thought it would be a good idea to write out prayers for use by the three young men trapped in Daniel's furnace. This apocryphal material, "Additions to Daniel," was not included in the Jewish Bible and some Protestant Bibles. It includes a confession of national sin and, of all things, a superb creation hymn. It is both a blessing of the Lord God and an apostrophe to all creation to participate in that blessing. Here is a portion of this not generally known text:

> **Bless the Lord,**
> **all you works of the Lord . . .**
> **Bless the Lord,**
> you heavens . . . you waters above the heavens. . ..
> **Bless the Lord,**
> sun and moon . . . stars of heaven . . . all rain and dew . . . all you winds...
> **Bless the Lord,**
> fire and heat . . . winter cold and summer heat . . .
> dews and snow. . . .

> Bless the Lord,
> days and nights . . . light and darkness...
> lightnings and clouds . . .
> Bless the Lord,
> all that grows in the ground . . .
> you springs
> Bless the Lord,
> you whales and all that swim . . .
> all birds of the air... wild animals.
> Bless the Lord,
> all people on earth . . .
> spirits and souls of the righteous. . .
> Bless the Lord,
> you who are holy and humble in heart. . .
> Bless the God of gods . . .
> and give thanks to him,
> for his mercy endures forever. [3]

The beat is insistent. The creator, not creation, is praised. The living, the dead and even the pagan gods are urged to join in praising *Yahweh*, the holy One of Israel.

Is this biblical tradition viable today? Has the modern passion for the mastery of creation for a variety of commercial, technological, scientific, political and military reasons closed this ancient door? Nature is no longer divine nor even an agency of the divine when it becomes understood only as an object subject to human manipulation. This obvious increase in human power carries with it a hidden, but certain, loss of human power at the same time. If we can relate to nature only as a collection of objects, does it not also reduce us humans, who are a part of nature, to being a mere assembly of objects ourselves? Materialism, popular or philosophical, seems to be the inevitable result. Does not the dehumanization of humanity become irresistible as well?

It is possible that the third of the great biblical meditations on the meaning and value of the physical universe provides grounds for an answer. It takes us from ancient Israel/Iraq to first century Turkey. Genesis portrayed God as a mid-Eastern monarch whose very utterances are immediately effective—thus demonstrating the power of language. "God said . . . and it was so." Words can achieve results—especially when it is God who is speaking. John's text is similar but not really identical. Here we hear not a series of spoken words. Here the word as such, communication, is God and does all the work.

In Genesis, creation begins in historical time, exactly on the first day of a seven day week. John drops that temporal sequence. Instead, the Gospel's first two verses imagine that God transcends everything that exists in space/ time. Not until the third verse does anything come into finite existence. Only then does creation start. The prologue dares speak, however briefly, of what is the context of space/time. It is divinity as communication, God's own self-communication. It is possible, John shows, to use words to point positively to an eternity which is not mere nothingness.

John's prologue appears to rest on both Hebrew and Greek antecedents. Proverbs 8:22-31 portrays wisdom as God's agent and instrument at the beginning of creation: "Ages ago (wisdom declares), I was set up at the first, before the beginning of the earth." This praise of God's use of wisdom in the origins of creation parallels the picture of God's use of language in Genesis. This use of wisdom in Proverbs is also similar if not identical to *logos*, the Greek designation for the principle of reason that enables the human mind to understand the natural world. The usual English translation of both the Greek *logos* and the Hebrew *dabar* as "word" implies a general equivalence. The prologue's use of *logos* implies both Hebrew and Greek antecedents. Out of eternity, this Gospel announces, God's self-communication (*logos*) brings a cosmos into being which is comprehensible in various ways. Eternity is the primordial context which brings into being a creation capable of participating in God's own light, grace and truth.

Whether John's Prologue was written in west Turkey or not, its writer probably would have known the substance of the narrative of the Sermon on the Mount.[4] Jesus offers there a wisdom teaching by speaking of the meaning of his Father's bountiful care and artistry in adorning the fields of Galilee with flowers and birds.

A problem some readers have had with John's prologue deserves comment. "How can the Word be both God and with God?" Actually, this is not an inherently paradoxical claim since even in ordinary speech existence and relationship are not inevitably contradictory.

In common speech, we expect people of integrity to be what they represent themselves to be. "I am what I say I am" is an unremarkable claim. A divine word and a divine being, are not two gods. When you are what you say you are, you are not two different beings. At the level of existential meaning, you are what you disclose yourself to be—in words and action. You can communicate yourself authentically.

A puzzling feature in this Gospel's elegant prologue are its two interruptions by that fierce prophet, John the Baptist. [5] There is no textual evidence that its writers saw this as a problem. It is more likely that they intended to give their Gospel a prologue that would identify three different but interconnected theaters of God's life: eternity, creation, and history. Eternity is the ultimate context in which God's word communicates the cosmos into existence. Creation demonstrates light and life springing into space from that same creative word. History is the theater in which three men interact with that word. Moses with his law, John with his late-in-time prophecy, and ultimately, the one in whom God's grace and truth shine forth for all humankind. These eighteen swiftly paced verses preview the whole sweep of this Gospel.

## Why Creation Matters

It might seem that finding the courage to believe in God would be better served if we could just forget about the world and all that is in it—at least until it comes crashing in on us, all uninvited. Many have said, and believed, that the earth is a distraction for people of faith. There is no lack of evidence to support that view. But the problem then is if religion is no earthly good, what good is it for those of us living in this world? It is quite possible to conceive of religion as an escape from the woes and temptations of the world. Whole religions, ancient and modern, have been based on that belief. Early Christianity, as it spread rapidly across the Greco-Roman world, sometimes took the shape of a Gnosticism which disparaged the world as the creation of an inept if not evil god and from which Christ had come to set humankind free. Creation of the world? No good god would fashion, much less, plunge into the filth of matter. Salvation is liberation from all things earthly. Unfortunately for the Gnostics the development of the biblical canons, old and new, made their demonization of creation theologically impossible.

A very different issue has proven a problem for Christian belief in modern times. The development of science since the eighteenth century has seemed to many to posit a world-view incompatible with that which the Bible assumes. A quick, if unreflective, response to that suspicion was to claim that traditional interpretations of the Bible have given all that we need: an eternal, final and absolute description of God's understanding of all matters scientific. Moses, the tradition's author of Genesis, would have to have been sufficiently inspired to be able to anticipate scientific knowledge not available otherwise to his generation. This belief in magic, totally absent in the biblical texts themselves, not only collided with contemporary research into the formation of the cosmos and all living things. It also required wholesale rejection of contemporary biblical scholarship. The deplorable consequences of this religious anti-intellectualism have infected not only the internal life of many religious communities but public education and the political life of whole nations.

Of course, Fundamentalism claims to be loyal to what it believes to be traditional. That desire is understandable, but it is purchased at the cost of clinging to vast ignorance about the formations of the cosmos and of the Bible itself. The courage to believe in God as creator requires something much more than affirming an anachronistic theory about prehistoric life. The gospel, we are told on good authority, is about a Father who is still at work. (6)

Why does creation have to matter for people of faith? The possible meanings of creation are innumerable. But this is crucial: Creation in all its mystery, its comprehensibility and incomprehensibility, its terror and vulnerability, its beauty, and vitality, is most of all a gift. It is not a human achievement nor a god nor an open book. It is gift of grace. We all start our lives believing that we've been given something and we demand to get more. A child's first cry for comfort and milk assumes that service is available. Babies are born expecting they can get what they need. "And right now, if you don't mind." Do we come, trailing clouds of glory? Or do we just want to get warm and fed? Or both? Actually, what could be more glorious when you are one day old than getting warm and fed in this cold and noisy world?

Babies may not get what they want. Many do not. But for them to be raised knowing that they have no reason to believe they will be cared for and loved, kept clean and fed, is a personal disaster. The world must mean something. It could mean, "Welcome, we're so glad that you could come." It may mean only "Stop crying. We're all only objects around here."

Fortunate children learn early that they can believe that the world they know is a gift that keeps on giving. Before they have words to name it, the experience of a positive relationship of trust between infant and caregiver is critically important. It may be neglected or betrayed, and that would be tragic. Later, when words do come, what should they say about needing to be welcomed, cared for, cleaned up, and fed?

It is significant that faith communities regularly seek to give children the gift of knowing that they are embraced by someone who cares. For example, in the long global history of Protestantism, the most widely used handbook for parents has made this very clear. Children are encouraged to ask, "What does it mean to believe that God is the Creator of all that exists?" The question is not about current geological research. It is a personal question about the meaning of that area of creation which the child knows most intimately. The answer for this is simply: "It means that I believe that God has given me my body and soul and reason along with all that is necessary for this body and life." [7]

Or is this the wrong answer? Why encourage Suzie to take herself so seriously?

A child's knowing that her immediate world is actually a gift makes possible for her to enter it—past, present, and future—in confidence. Being able to understand even a part of creation is a gift. What is foundational for human intelligence is not the latest scientific understanding of the origins of the cosmos. What matters initially for human life is an awareness by its subjects that this is a context that can be trusted. A child's frail but fierce subjectivity is where we all have to begin. Is that a regrettable bias which, try as we will, we can never truly overcome? Or is recognizing it not the indispensible if humbling part of learning how to deal with the limitations and powers of all human knowing?

As Suzie grows in years and wisdom she will become increasingly aware of the connections between those powers and limitations. If she is fortunate, she will be connected to communities in which creation is regarded not just as a dumb fact, but as an awe-inspiring gift, an unfailing source of wonder which we only partly understand and yet for which we are ultimately responsible. All of us are fortunate that in today's world there are many communities in which respect for data and wonder are permitted to co-exist, communities in which religious faith and scientific understanding have learned how to engaged in dialogue.

## The Environment

While the old controversy between science and religion has often been characterized as a fight that has left the latter hanging on the ropes, it turns out that the struggle is not quite over. Something's stirring. As in every apparently successful enterprise, sooner or later someone starts to ruin things by poking around and asking awkward ethical questions. Here are a few:

- *Why is more technology—an applied science—always assumed to be a good thing? Are the deciders responsible only to themselves—or to no one? How can that be ethical? Who gets to decide what's good for all of us?*
- *Has science's technical brilliance in developing nuclear weapons made the world more or less secure? Is their value based on anything other than their psychological power to make people afraid?*
- *Does not global warming potentially endanger all sentient life on the planet? Among people, why is it permissible that it is the children, the aged, and the poor who are required to pay the heaviest price?*
- *Is Christianity generally irrelevant or indifferent to the natural environment?*
- *Is it politically possible for industrial development to become ecologically responsible? If it is not, why is combating global warming meeting with massive political resistance?*

What questions would you add?

When creation is believed to be a continuing sign of grace, it is not enough just to praise its author for it. Appreciation for a gift is best measured by the quality of care which the gift receives. Regarding nature, even in its strangeness, as a neighbor to be loved has come to be seen as an ethical imperative in our time. Ethics-as-ecological-responsibility is now a growth industry. Three areas are particularly promising:

*(a) There are, of course, wide differences in basic beliefs among the world religions. Efforts to turn their doctrinal discord into harmony have proven less than encouraging. But what is striking in interreligious dialogue is an increasing consensus that stresses the importance of the moral responsibility for the physical environment. The groundbreaking 1990 Middlebury College symposium on "Spirit and Nature" representing Iroquois, Jewish, Muslim, Unitarian, Buddhist, and Christian (as well as feminist, artistic and political science) perspectives proved an influential example.*[8] World religions have been shown to be acutely aware of the relevance of their spiritualities for the care of the earth. The very multiplicity of their voices has strengthened their shared witness What may be more important is the challenge of that witness for each tradition to rethink its history and future.

*(b) Among Christians, God's work in nature is celebrated as a sign of divine majesty and care for all. In the past that awareness has been publically expressed mostly in its liturgies and hymnody. Creation is receiving increasing prominence in both.*[9] *A breakthrough in American theological circles was the 1962 publication of two books in one by George H. Williams under the title* **Wilderness and Paradise in Christian Thought: The Biblical Experience of the Desert in the History of Christianity and The Paradise Theme in the Theological Idea of the University**. *As an historian, Williams showed how the Christian narrative is deeply involved in two seemingly unrelated contexts: untamed nature and higher education.*[10] *Four years latter, Lynn White Jr., an Episcopalian layman and professor of history at the University of California, Berkley, in an address before the American Academy for the Advancement of Science, charged that "Christianity bears a huge burden of guilt" for the disastrous consequences of modern technology's manipulation of basic life forms. The popular media and many environmentalists quickly agreed—to the dismay of academics in the religious community. Five years later, a group of Christian intellectuals, who thought otherwise offered a multiple-disciplined, wide-ranging response,* **A New Ethic for a New Earth**. [11]*As sometimes happens, the controversy proved salutary. Subsequently a flood of biblical, doctrinal and ethical volumes have been published, a sign of the seriousness with which Christians have become environmentally concerned.* [12]

*(c) Philosophers, too, have been seriously engaged in addressing today's environmental crisis. Particularly well done is Roderick Frazier Nash's* **The Rights of Nature: A History of Environmental Ethics**, *a survey of the changing attitudes toward nature in American history that also shows how an ethics of liberation can be expanded to address nature as well as humanity.*[13] *Holmes Rolston's lucid philosophical analysis of key issues in his* **Environmental Ethics: Duties to and Values in the Natural World** *seeks to bridge the gap between commerce and natural rights ethicists.*[14] *His strategy is to ask whether moral values are immanent in nature. If so, what, if any, are our moral duties to sentient life, to endangered species, indeed, to the whole*

*ecosystem? He finds responsibility for the well-being of the planet requires belief in an ethical transcendence emergent in nature and moving us beyond the limitations of strictly humanistic thought. In fact, moral responsibility makes it necessary to move beyond liberalism's traditional preoccupation with human life. He recalls approvingly Victor Hugo's charge, "It is also necessary to civilize humans in relation to nature. There, everything remains to be done."*[15] *Bryan Norton's robust ethical basis for environmentalism reflects more than a species-centric humanism is prepared to allow. In his epilogue he acknowledges that environmentalists ... must admit that the creativity of nature is the Great Mystery... (It) was the prophetic (John) Muir who recognized most clearly that science and theology would eventually merge once again as they did in Genesis I. The linchpin of the modern environmental movement is the belief that the study of nature has this ecstatic aspect: the ability to inspire wonder at our 'partness,' and at the whole of which we are a part, is simply an object of contemplation, not exploitation. If that were to occur, environmentalists believe, there would be more support for contextually sensitive policies."* [16]

Robert S. Corrington's *Nature's Self: Our Journey from Origin to Spirit* is sympathetic to Norton's interest in reconnecting science to religion.[17] His study is an ontological exploration of the tensions between human finitude in nature on one hand and human connections to a "fitful transcendence," i.e. an ecstatic naturalism that bears a striking resemblance to voices in classical theology. Arran E. Gare's *"Postmodernism and the Environmental Crisis"* is a brilliant exposé of the failures of modern intellectual, political, and popular cultures to address the ecological realities of our time.[18] Anthony Weston's *An Invitation to Environmental Philosophy* presents five different author's reflections on key ethical issues, a fine introduction to the field. [19] Studies such as these provide the context for understanding the religious significance of creation. But the gorilla in the living room is something new. What does the undoubted success of Charles Darwin's achievement in today's scientific culture mean for the religions of the world?

## Evolution

Scientists have argued that whatever value Genesis may have, its accounts of creation cannot be "literally true." That obvious attack on traditional religion appeared to be supported when, also in the nineteenth century, academics began to claim that apart from its content, the literary formation of the Bible needs to be understood as a complex multi-cultural historical development. For the most part, both of these challenges to tradition were at first vigorously resisted. That opposition is still active, but it has lost the crucially important, authoritative support of the theological leadership in Protestant, Catholic, and Jewish communities.

How could that have happened? Its origins were literary, not scientific. In the nineteenth century, increasing numbers of biblical scholars began to be convinced that an accurate interpretation of sacred texts requires a reconstruction of the historical context in which the writers lived. If readers do not do that difficult but not impossible work, they will inevitably end up doing *eisegesis* instead of *exegesis*. Instead of the text being a window into the mind of the writer, it becomes only a mirror darkly reflecting the mind of the reader. That may be psychologically reassuring. But it distorts, if not silences, the voice of the writer.

Attending to historical contexts is particularly important when it comes to reading the biblical accounts of creation. Since different texts have different contexts, ignoring those contexts actually disrespects and obscures the writers' achievement. Why assume that the diversity among the creation accounts is a theological problem? Is it not rather testimony to the continuing creative vitality of a very long tradition in its historical development? As we have already seen in the work of the priestly writers during the exile, and then in the Johannine community at the end of the first century, traditional beliefs in the Creator could be challenged and transformed as new understandings of the scope of creation became compelling. Israelite priests found how a judicious use of elements native to Babylonian mythology could significantly expand the older *Yahwist* account. Five hundred years later, Jewish Christians in Turkey saw that their mission to the world would be credible only if they could show how their understanding of creation could connect and challenge the much larger world in which they lived. Both communities demonstrated that fidelity to religious traditions need not make them flee from new experience. This kind of religious imagination was not unheard of. The Scriptures had made it impossible for them to forget Abraham, the definitive exemplar of the root meaning of faith. The Abraham story showed that faith is an act of obedience understood as a bold openness to *Yahweh's* purposes; it would lead God's people into an unknown future. [20] The question before students in the twenty-first century is whether today's profoundly new understandings of the nature of the cosmos can again be permitted to expand (and be expanded by) these ancient biblical traditions.

What happens when theologians dare think about evolution?

More than a half-century ago, Teilhard de Chardin published the French edition of *The Phenomenon of Man*,[21] aptly described by a German scholar as "a new synthesis of evolution." [22] Teilhard was certainly not the first theologian to attempt to coordinate biblical and scientific thinking. But as a Jesuit priest and a paleontologist, he was deeply concerned that his synthesis be not only religiously faithful but scientifically responsible  Far from evolution being a problem for religion, he believed it to be the key for understanding the basic coherence of nature and spirit. While the immediate response to his work voiced both scientific and theological skepticism, over time his kind of  advocacy for evolutionary thinking has proven increasingly attractive among Catholics and Protestants.

## Science and Theology

Knowing what it is that you are to believe about creation has become increasingly difficult in the twenty-first century. Scientific understandings of the scope of the natural world—what's out there, what's in here—has become for the non-specialist virtually incomprehensible. How can any individual be expected to understand the range between the galaxies billions of light years out there as well as the atomic structures of the human brain in here engaged in attempting to comprehend those galaxies?

That's not all. The astonishing growth of the power of science in its capacity for investigation as well as in its technological applications, we are assured, will increase exponentially in the future.

And that's still not all. The twenty-first century will witness the stress of having to provide space for a variety of world cultures, some of which will embrace, and some of which will resist, this increasing power of science and technology.

How will the religions fare? Some, if not most, will find it necessary to oppose the increasing hegemony of scientific thinking. Many Christians will be caught up in confusions about what to think, what to do. Will theology make their problems worse? Or, will it recover its native vocation: to show how faith leads to wisdom, how ignorance is the way of the wicked? But is it really only the religious who are ignorant?

Religions which have no interest in the physical universe and choose to focus exclusively on an otherworldly silent Other, One quite uncontaminated by engagement with the contingencies of space and time, will seem to have a strategic advantage here. This, however, has proven not a viable option for those difficult twins, Judaism and Christianity, and their younger sister Islam, unless they become willing to abandon their traditional beliefs about God's acting in nature and human history. That possibility is proposed by the Gnostics from time to time, but it early proved to be an anomaly, fundamentally inconsistent with both Torah and gospel in canon and creed. Genesis and John begin with brief but strong accounts of a creation that is temporal, contingent, not necessary and not everlasting. Later, the ecumenical creeds begin not with a word about Christ, but with an affirmation of the divine source of creation. This belief is also basic to Judaism and Islam and is at least similar to the beliefs expressed in indigenous religions as well. Aboriginal peoples invoke the presence of the divine in dance and song. In their rites they hail the power and wonder of divinity encountered everywhere in the natural world. In prayer the community spontaneously connects to an unseen spiritual world. A few of the indigenous religions are still with us.[24] But what could be more foreign to these ancient witnesses to the sanctity of nature than the world described by modern cosmology? Even small children in privileged societies quickly notice this discrepancy. Does this mean that as the authority of science grows, all memory of the sacred as enshrined in canon and creed will be doomed to obsolescence? Must modernity result in an ethnic/religious cleansing that will eliminate the surviving indigenous peoples and their beliefs?

This crisis is relatively new. It was not a problem for the biblical writers or the great theologians of the past, patristics, medievals, and reformers. Irenenus, Augustine, Thomas Aquinas and Martin Luther all faced a wide range of new issues raised by the cultures of their time. But crafting a durable doctrine of creation was not particularly difficult for them since secular as well as sacred literature had made free use of what modern writers commonly describe as "mythical modes of discourse" They certainly were not expected to do the unimaginable: crafting a doctrine of creation that would somehow anticipate twenty-first century cosmologies.

Our situation today is very different. It certainly has become a problem for believers who cannot but notice that the Bible in keeping with the cultures of the times of its origins makes liberal use of "mythical styles of language." The problem of using such speech, especially in its reference to creation, has been felt with special force since the eighteenth century. What was an issue for a few intellectuals then has become an issue for virtually every religious person today. Is it not the obligation of faith to meet these new challenges and learn from them? Or, is it better to try to avoid difficult problems?

Understanding the religious significance of creation has many forms. Since the eighteenth century two issues have become prominent. One is semantic, the other philosophical. The former lies in the confusion regarding our use of the word "myth." Standard dictionaries preserve this ambiguity. "Myth" can refer to the classical legends of ancient peoples: Persians and Hebrews, Greeks and Indians, Romans and Germans, Nordics and Africans. Ancient peoples developed a wealth of narratives for interpreting the meanings of their natural environment, the social order, their spiritual identity and destiny. Anthropologists and psychiatrists have marveled at the creativity and profundity of much of this material. These Myths are treasures from the ancient past, at least as valuable as a collection of ancient sculptures at the Metropolitan Museum. Let the capitalized word Myth be our term for these rightly treasured legends.

On the other hand, "myth" has a dark side. It also means a common but false belief, something untrue but uncritically accepted as true. We are stuck with this ambiguity, not unlike confusions created by other words that have double, sometimes contradictory, meanings: e.g. man, Indian, America. This is a problem for anyone looking for a non-prejudicial assessment of religion. For centuries it has been clear that the legends of ancient religions are not scientific accounts. Are they, then, simply untrue? Perhaps the best strategy would be to let the word "myth" continue to decay into this popular second meaning as something false as we try to find a new word or phase for the first meaning. Perhaps "legend, or "saga" or "traditional symbolic account" would work. Perhaps not. For purposes of the present discussion, "Myth" (upper case) is used for the first, academic, literary meaning while "myth" (lower case) is used for the second, meaning a commonly accepted bit of fiction as though it were true. To speak of biblical texts of creation as traditional symbolic accounts does not prejudge their veracity. To call them myths certainly does. In academic contexts it is clear that the authority of these texts is not scientific but cultural, i.e., moral and philosophical. Mythological language is universal in antiquity, a language people today need to be able to understand and if they wish to gain access to their own origins. Again we see that fluency in more than one language is essential for knowledge.

The second problem is philosophical. It is caught up in the belief common since the eighteenth century that the credibility of God's "existence" is dependent on one's being able to prove that God is the author of creation. No proof: no God. Upon reflection, that seems odd since none of the biblical writers, for example, seems to regard the problem of what Europeans mean by "existence" as a subject worthy of attention. Power, justice, mercy, presence, holiness, mystery, passion, creativity, freedom, identity are the realities of revelation. But whether or not society as a whole has (or I in my solitary reflections have) the intellectual power to define—and thus capture—the meaning of that puzzling abstraction, "existence" was not on the agenda. Should it be? Plato was certain that truth exists. How could someone know that it is true to say that anything in particular exists if truth itself does not exist? Would it be possible to live in a world in which goodness does not exist prior to our coming into it? Is beauty only a biological strategy? Classical philosophers found all three—truth, goodness, and beauty—to transcend any specific instance of them. That they exist is certain. That their existence is not empirically provable is obvious.

Finally, whose definition (or assumption) about "existence" counts as provable? Can we prove our own existence? Descartes' readers have pointed out that he has not proven that "I think, therefore I am" since the subject of "am" has already been smuggled in as the unproven subject of "think." Well, then, are we stuck with believing that our existence rests on what we *chose* to believe?" How would that work? Do you have to prove to yourself that your beloved exists before you let yourself fall in love? Would your lover find this insulting or, mercifully, just laugh at you? Beyond all this, does everything we know or experience "exist" in the same way?

The third problem is the relation of religion to science. Until the middle of the nineteenth century, it was commonly believed as self evident that the world was created by God. [25] The concern, of course, was not on how God did this. What mortal could possibly know that? The point was that the world had not made itself. It was God, not some devil or dumb luck, that had brought the world into being. That assumption was not trivial. The philosophical value of the traditional assumption was its power to engender a profound emphasis on the worth, reality and order of the world. That assumption has shown to have had incalculable consequences. Among them were cosmological presuppositions validating confidence in the high value of the natural world and the consequent moral responsibility of humankind to take care of it. These traditional beliefs were common in the scientific community "from Galileo through Newton, Priestley, Ray, Dalton, Boyle and Thomas Burnett even down to Linnaeus and Cuvier." [26] Scientists also generally assumed that a religious understanding of creation was in harmony with the research they were conducting. Two corollaries followed: Creation's forms and structures were universal and purposefully designed by the wisdom of the creator. And the creation of the earth was relatively recent.

Geological studies in the eighteenth century brought disturbing dissonance into this consensus. More time, much more time, it came to be seen, was necessary to account for the history of the earth than the 6,000 years that some biblical scholars had proposed. Fossil remains of animals now extinct and evidence of vast changes in the Earth itself suggested that the "Book of Nature" and the "Book of the Word" were incommensurate. As La Place famously pointed out, a materialist belief that nature is only "matter in motion," makes it unnecessary to posit a divinity to fill in the gaps in scientific knowledge. Other scientists, however, continued to labor to find evidence for a supernatural agency in the natural order.

But what if LaPlace were right? Would not the best procedure be to replace theology with philosophical proposals based not on ancient myths but on science? As the evidence for evolution proved increasingly persuasive, it was asked whether the process of evolution could not be assigned at least some of the roles previously assumed by deity. In England, distinguished atheists such as T. H. Huxley believed that this held much promise. And on the continent, materialists such as Friedrich Nietzsche found that the evolutionary struggle for survival could easily be pressed to serve as a "scientific basis" for an explicitly anti-Christian ethic of power. Karl Marx and his followers showed how history could be seen in terms of a scientific materialism that would usher in a godless utopia of justice for some, but certainly not for the shopkeepers and clergy. In the twentieth century, the planet became a world-wide, extravagant laboratory preoccupied with testing the consequences of these philosophers' beliefs. The laboratory, as we now know, turned out to be an abattoir.

At the beginning of the twenty-first century, the West suddenly confronted an unexpected challenge.[27] How could the futurologists have been so mistaken? How could a medieval *religion*, of all things, suddenly prove so powerful? The materialist bias of the West had made it seem necessary to see the Muslim world in purely secular terms. The West's dismissal of its own religious past had been projected globally. It was believed that world affairs are determined by power politics, international economics and effective military strategies—not by some dated, incomprehensible sectarian disputes.

The problem however is that Islam does not believe this. It believes that religion and culture cannot be separated. It believes that the West became not merely post-Christian in the twentieth century, but post-religious. If a society no longer believes that God is the creator of all that exists, then the Koran has been rejected. There then would be no longer a shared belief in an ultimate justice and divine compassion for humankind--as the Koran teaches. Everything would be thrown into chaos. What greater disaster could befall the world? Muslims are not afraid of the West. They know that whatever the cost, they will never be defeated in their struggle against the West's shocking infidelity, its practical atheism.

The struggle between Islam and the West may become the next chapter in the West's two-century- old problem with atheism, but it is more than that. The planet which modern technology has made so very small is peopled by many good and wise and beautiful and crowded people. But, in the West at least, we no longer commonly believe that we are deeply, ultimately accountable for what we do to the world and to ourselves. We can no longer decide whether we need to believe in the presence of a sacred goodness in ourselves, in each other and in the world. Why is this? Because there is no longer a way open for us to come to a common mind as to whether there is any ultimate goodness available for all. Goodness is now merely a private affair and is available only for those who have access to the somewhat unpredictable market.

Today's problem comes down to this: if we agree that the world is godless either because we believe that there is no God, or because we cannot find the courage to believe in a God whom we cannot transcend by virtue of our superior knowledge, the outcome is the same. We will then live out our lives isolated from any conscious contact with the sacred in ourselves and in the rest of the human family. We are unaware of our ultimate connectedness.

This does not mean that the sacred has no contact with us. It just means that our receivers are turned off. It means that since we have found no unbidden beauty invading our own lives, we can not conceive of a beauty beyond us-- in the wildness of a Canadian winter, in the swift plunge of a South African shark or in solving a problem in algebra. Beauty, like all values, is but a projection. What you see is what you make, what you construe.

There are no gifts, only purchases.

Since it appears that the consequences of not being able to resolve any number of social, aesthetic, or philosophical obstacles to belief in the sacred substance of creation are considerable, what should we to do? Are there any options for moving ahead to a knowledge of creation that connects it to holiness? Actually, there are.

## Literalism

Literalism has shown remarkable resilience. The biblical authors and the patristics, medievals, and reformers freely used interpretive models such as metaphor, allegory, poetry and parable in their work. But particularly since the rise of modern science, some religious leaders have sought to reject such strategies especially with reference to Genesis and some areas of ethics. The argument: If there is a collision between science and the Bible, the latter must have the last word. An infallible Bible, perfect in all its parts and as a whole, is required for maintaining the primacy of God and the dignity of humankind. Some would hold that the six days of creation could be interpreted to refer to much longer time periods. But true conservatives understandably regard such a concession as a tampering with the sacred text and therefore impermissible. The alert reader will note that the biblical writers themselves do not present such an extraordinary position. Indeed, it is not unfair to note that this position is profoundly at odds with the way later portions of the Bible regularly engage in the reinterpretation of the earlier texts. So why does literalism enjoy significant support?

The power and popularity of biblical literalism is not informed by theological sensitivity. Its roots are partly psychological: access to an infallible book can remove doubt and uncertainty. They are also political: Taken out of context, it is possible to find something somewhere in the Bible that can be used to offer divine support for whatever notion is politically necessary. Worst of all, literalism is an abuse of the sacred, an act of idolatry. There is a ready remedy for it however: cultivate a deep respect for these rich ancient texts by approaching them in a spirit of honesty and humility.

Fortunately, other alternatives beckon.

## Fences Make Good Neighbors

In recent years, philosophers of religion, of language, and of science as well as theologians have addressed the science/religion issue. Each discipline has its own canons and seeks to respect those of its partners. Would a strategy of dialogue be worth trying? Theologians in the twentieth century began by emphasizing the differences between theological and scientific research. In brief: neither discipline should be absorbed by the other. Imperialism is as toxic in the academy as it is geo-politically—probably for the same reasons. Using widely different arguments, major Protestant voices developed magisterially comprehensive systems that made conflict between religion and science impossible. The major figures were Karl Barth and Paul Tillich.

Barth decisively rejected all forms of "natural theology," especially a theology based on the outrageous but politically popular theory of the biological superiority of a particular twentieth century European nation. Christian theology, Barth insisted, is entirely a theology of the Word, i.e. the revelation of God in Israel and Christ. Science is designed to analyze the natural world, but is not competent to assess divine revelation. [28]

Tillich's correlation of ontology and existentialism achieved similar results but in a very different way. Theology's use of ontology and existentialism makes a collision with natural science epistemologically impossible. Example: It is critically important that scientists be detached, rigorously objective, in their attitude toward their subjects. It is just as important that theologians and artists not be detached but personally engaged, grasped by the "spiritual presence" of their subjects. [29] Questions?

*a. How would these attempts to separate theology from science affect the way we read the Bible?*

Both Barth and Tillich understood their work to rest on the Protestant Reformation's restatement of the doctrine of revelation:

The content of revelation is not an historically conditioned body of antique texts describing the nature of God, but a unique narrative concerning persons who in their life story bear witness to having received a message of transcendent judgment and grace. The Bible in all its diversity and historical particularity is the indispensible record of that message. It employs the literary forms and cultural traditions that were currently available. But they are not the content of the message. It would be idolatry to regard them as such.

*b. How does this relate to science?*

Science is usually thought to deal with "finite causal relationships within the temporal process." Religion, however, deals with the meaning of historical experience as well as the value and significance of the world as a cosmic process. Thus the popular, casual twining of the words "creation" and "nature" interchangeably is theologically misleading. "Nature" properly refers to the origins of life on earth and of the structure of the cosmos, while "creation" refers to the value and meanings of the world's history in relation to God's self disclosure. The two disciplines engage the world from two different perspectives. Both strategies are valid.

*c. How does this affect what is meant by the word "God?"*

A theology based on the biblical canon reflects on the meaning of what God has done in events of transcendent holiness. These events are embedded in a richly patterned narrative, simultaneously naïve and profound in its unvarnished multi-cultural, multi-lingual testimony. A tension-filled dialectic is characteristic: God and the world are intimately related but they are not equal partners. God is inescapable yet radically different from the world which assumes, falsely, that it is everlasting. God is transcendent and ultimate, yet characteristically personal, passionate and vulnerable. God is unique, and in a derivative way, so too are the innumerable individuals who gather into particular communities to celebrate their wonder-filled adventures in worlds sacred and profane. Even in their struggles, sorrows and defeats they have been caught up, they say, into the life, love and light of holiness.

d. *What does this have to do with the character of the creation?*

The Hebrew and Greek texts speak freely of the providential goodness which embraces all creation. This goodness sustains the physical world, stars and fish, the sinners and the just. Over the centuries, this affirmation has often been weakened and sometimes repudiated under pressure from idealistic dualisms which contrast the physical (evil) and the spiritual (divine). In the contemporary world, religious ethicists and artists have sought to recover the older tradition as an invaluable resource in efforts to arouse ecological sensitivity as well as to stimulate environmental responsibility. The pre-scientific language used by the biblical texts rule out their being sources for natural science today. But when they are used as intended, i.e. as an invitation to a life of justice and love, they can powerfully strengthen the resolve to defend nature from human abuse. They can address us. They can condemn and inspire. They can stoke the fires of moral passion urgently needed for protecting this fragile, natural world.

e. *Intellectuals, politicians, CEOs, and clergy have their special myths. Do scientists?*

Langdon Gilkey pointed out a strange problem. The scientific community characteristically sees itself as uncompromisingly committed to belief (!) that its own work is a free "act of human creative rational autonomy." [30] Yet, scientific answers to questions about humankind "always present to us a picture of a determined creature whose rise, organizational structure, functions and powers are exhaustively explained within the terms of the casual nexus." The data gained are highly informative, but do not provide a way to justify our using this scientific language for distinctively human purposes. Efforts to use such knowledge as a basis for any "transformative activity" that implies human freedom, dignity and moral responsibility collapse into mere opinion. In practice, scientific knowledge moves inexorably in the direction of total determinism.

*f. Is science then the enemy of democracy? Is the struggle for power within the scientific community not an act of human freedom? If it is, how can the scientific community understand itself strictly "scientifically" rather than politically or humanistically?*

Actually the scientific community has often championed human freedom, dignity and moral responsibility. But such values are pre-scientific and were borrowed from the philosophical history of the West which borrowed them from the writings of ancient Jews, Greeks, and early Christians. Academic communities insist on the freedom of teachers and students to pursue the truth. They should. But believing in that freedom is a demanding act of faith. That faith is by no means rationally self evident and risk free.

*g. Does science (and its derivatives, engineering and technology) have its own myths?*

When science is used in socially responsible ways, it is indispensible for the progress of society. But, of course "social responsibility" is not a technologically meaningful concept. The academy commonly believes that it is essential for society to provide strong support for scientific and technological work. This belief is assumed at all levels of science education. It also holds that the manipulation of nature by medical, biological, and engineering science will protect and enrich human life. The breathtaking optimism of this belief is striking. Who decides what's best for society if that cannot be determined scientifically? What criteria does the scientific community use in making its non-scientific ethical choices?

In today's world, it is increasingly clear that the human manipulation of nature has had horrific consequences: global climate change, pollution of the air and seas, development of atomic and nuclear weapons, increasing global poverty and the Holocaust. Not surprisingly, a dystopian apocalypticism has become a dominant form of entertainment among the technologically savvy young. Albert Einstein is not the only physicist to worry about the human willingness to use technological power for morally catastrophic ends.

The attempt to solve these kinds of problems has become a dominant theme of contemporary culture. Perhaps all will be solved and in the long run we'll all be better off. But not, of course, in our life time. The belief that as humankind has an increasing capacity to control nature, it will be sure to exercise that power benignly for the benefit of all, or at least for the greatest number, generally goes unchallenged. No religious doctrine receives the support which this myth enjoys. No religious illusion has ever been less credible or more dangerous.

The optimistic myth of humankind's natural ability and willingness to bend power to serve goodness for the benefit of all is a central dogma in contemporary Western culture. Historically, it is relatively recent and bears no obvious relation to the experience of humankind. Would Christianity's insistence on the importance for non-prejudicial, non-defensive self-criticism (classically known as the doctrine of original sin) be of help? Would learning to doubt modernity's flattering belief in its own virtue be an insightful first step? Or is that belief secure regardless of the evidence? Are we really intellectually incorrigible?

*h. Are technology and morality related?*

Technology is indeed intended to give humankind greater power over nature including human nature. That is understood as an act of freedom. But as it succeeds, it actually threatens freedom. As technology advances, it builds on its past successes which take on a life of its own. No executive, corporate or political, can stop technological advance. Technicians the world over are at work. A breakthrough here is quickly adopted there. Technology is a global system. But who is in control? [31] Information technology has made a highly sophisticated global economics inevitable. But there is no consensus as to how it can be used to achieve globally appropriate ends. Where then is humanity's moral accountability?

It is hard to see how the lack of human control of technological advance results in an advance in human freedom, if freedom has anything to do with autonomy. Financially secure individuals have an increasing range of choices. Yet some say that they are overwhelmed by the sheer quantity of choices. At the other end of the market, fewer choices are financially possible. While food or education or health care are theoretically possible, they are beyond the reach of increasing numbers of the world's population. The point, of course, is not to blame technology. At one time the farmer's hoe was a technological breakthrough. The problem is not the existence of tools. The problem is that the tools have become the masters. Tools can have minds, some say, but do tools have compassion? The record of power without compassion is a narrative of the abolition of freedom.

*i. Do the scientific and religious communities have anything in common?*

To demonize either religion or science is easy but childish. In mature societies both communities need to be to free to critique and enrich each other. Each needs to accept responsibility for the great evils done in its name. Each needs to explore how to engage the virtues of passion and humility, how to insist on its own integrity, how to find ways to serve the common good, and most of all each needs to find the courage to believe-- that they can actually do this.

## But a Cyclone Fence Is Not a Wall of Stone

Is there a third option? You may want to respond to the traditions of Barth and Tillich by asking: "Why dismiss Aquinas' magisterial attempt to combine "nature" (i.e. Aristotle) with "grace" (i.e. Paul) into a single, coherent cathedral of knowledge?" You may also want to point out that distinctions need not be separations. Bilingual people know that there's not just one way to say anything completely.

So perhaps the time is coming when science and religion will move into a kingdom of reconciliation. That time has not yet come. But theologically trained scientists—and scientifically trained theologians are working on it. British academics have been particularly interested in the exploring possible connections in the new work in the physical and social sciences, on one hand, and the philosophy of religion and biblical studies on the other. Whether this project will prove successful it is too early to say. It is certainly due close attention. Particularly noteworthy is the work of John Polkinghorne of Queens' College, Cambridge who has prepared an accessible overview for the general public in his *Science & Theology*.[32] His discussion of the "scientific picture of the world" will be particularly helpful for non-scientists trying to find out what quantum mechanics, modern cosmology and chaos theory are all about. The late Arthur Peacocke, formerly of Clare College, Cambridge and Saint Cross College, Oxford, published a larger study in his Gifford Lectures project which seeks to connect science, philosophy and classic theology by the construction of bridges between "natural being and becoming" and "divine being and becoming."[33]

The effort to build metaphysical bridges between science and religion is, of course, not new. When the English translation of Teilhard de Chardin's *The Phenomenon of Man* appeared in 1959, a sympathetic critic wrote that this "publication event of the year" would still be of interest a decade or two into the future. He was, of course, too reserved. The book has become an essential text for any reader today who is interested in seeing how a synthesis of the gospel and science might look. Aquinas' historic attempt to combine nature and grace as a third option is attracting renewed attention.

Modern poets have not been reluctant to explore ways in which creation and grace may meet. In his *Seven Odes to Seven Natural Processes,* the late John Updike tells us how intelligent our "mute brute body" is and how eager it is to heal us.[34] Do we, however, know what is health's requisite? You need to read his poem aloud.

## ODE TO HEALING

A scab
is a beautiful thing—a coin
the body has minted, with an invisible motto:
In God We Trust.
Our body loves us,
and, even while the spirit drifts dreaming,
works at mending the damage that we do.
That heedless Ahab the conscious mind
drives our thin-skinned hull onto the shoals;
a million brilliant microscopic engineers below
shore up the wound with platelets,
lay down the hardening threads of fibrin,
send in the lymphocytes, and supervise
those cheery swabs, the macrophages, in their clean-up.
Break a bone, and fibroblasts
knit tight the blastema in days.
Catch a cold, and the fervid armies
swarm to blanket our discomfort in sleep.
For all these centuries of fairy tales poor men
butchered each other in the name of cure,
not knowing an iota of what the mute brute body knew.
Logically, benevolence surrounds us.
In fire or ice, we would not be born.
Soft tissue bespeaks a soft world.
Yet, can it have been malevolence
that taught the skinned knuckle to heal
or set the white scar on my daughter's glossy temple?

Besieged, we are supplied,
from caustic saliva down,
with armaments against the hordes,
"the slings and arrows," "the thousand natural shocks."
Not quite benevolence.
Not quite its opposite.
A perfectionism, it would almost seem,
stuck with matter's recalcitrance,
as, in the realm of our behavior, with
the paradox of freedom.
Well, can we add a cubit to our height
or heal ourselves by taking conscious thought?
The spirit sits as a bird singing
high in a grove of hollow trees whose red sap rises
saturated with advice.
To the child as he scuffles up an existence
out of pebbles and twigs
and finds that even paper cuts, and games can hurt,
the small assemblage of a scab
is like the slow days' blurring of a deep disgrace,
the sinking of a scolding into time.
Time heals; not so;
time is the context of forgetting and of remedy
as aseptic phlegms
lave the scorched membranes,
the capillaries and insulted nerves.
Close your eyes, knowing
that healing is a work of darkness,
that darkness is a gown of healing,
that the vessel of our tremulous venture is lifted
by tides we do not control.
Faith is health's requisite:
we have this fact in lieu
of better proof of *le bon Dieu.*

Ancient poets gave the first lines in Scripture to praise God's goodness in creation. Poets still do so. Updike explores a strange, dark, divine goodness at work in nature around us and within, a goodness seeking the redemption of our bodies.

## CHAPTER FIVE

## *The Jesus Question*

The pivot in the oldest of the Gospels is a discussion of just who Jesus is.

The geographical setting for the episode is provocative. Still visible today is evidence that in earlier times Caesarea Philippi had been a center for pagan worship. Up there at the headwaters of the Jordan, people had been asking, "Who are the gods?" Mark says that when Jesus came, he pressed a similar point. "Who do you say that I am?" he asked. Peter, as usual, was quick to respond, but Jesus judged his answer to be only partly correct. The rest was an outrage: "Get behind me, Satan!" [1]

What we do know is that Jesus' foes and friends have always given all sorts of answers to his question. Many of them have been preserved in the New Testament: Son of Man, Son of God, Messiah, Lord, as well as drunkard, sinner, lunatic, Son of Satan, Son of Joseph. The terms affirming him are mostly idiomatic. That is, their meanings were common in first century Jewish culture, but usually are not well understood today. [2]

The question of the identity of Jesus has become a perennial theme in religious and secular history. Pelikan has shown that two millennia have generated at least eighteen creative and often highly effective answers to Jesus' question.[3] These cross-cultural engagements with the New Testament's pictures of Christ have not been efforts at repristination nor a rejection of the first century's achievement. A critical understanding of these influential, powerful and dangerous representations of Christ is far more important for believers than it could ever be for the skeptics. Although much of the controversy concerning Jesus' identity among both believers and non-believers has been revived in our time, something new has happened too. We are learning that Jesus' question can be significant not merely for reviving old polemics, but for the sake of discovering what those controversies may have missed. Probably we don't know as much as we thought we did.

Jesus and his first interpreters were first century Jews, all agree. Would building on that obvious foundation give not only an interesting, but the decisive, perspective for discerning Jesus' identity? That, after all, is where the action began. All else is but commentary. The early controversy about Jesus' relation to Israel which Paul in Romans 9-11 found so appalling needs not stand as an ugly concrete wall forever separating the people of God from themselves. Perhaps here too we could dare say someday, "Tear down this wall." This is the community, after all, that claims that God works miracles.

The point at which we should begin our search for Jesus' identity is not the compiling of a list of our personal or social problems to see how he just might fit in. Nor should we press the hopeless attempt to disengage Jesus and his first interpreters from their world—admittedly very foreign to our own—in an effort to make them our contemporaries. To make them appear relevant by transforming their passions into our own is to disrespect their particularity as well as a futile effort to avoid addressing our own. Do we want to be able to feel comfortable by succeeding in efforts to portray Jesus as someone just like ourselves? False comfort.

It would be more difficult and more honest to calm down and try to listen to what Jesus and his friends were saying. Much of it inevitably echoed the piety, morality and wisdom of first century religion (technically Second Temple Judaism). But is that the whole story? Did Jesus not have his own identity? If the Jesus movement were simply conventional, why would it have mattered? As a modern rabbi has perceptively observed, "the most revolutionary words of Jesus are these five: 'But I say unto you.'" This awareness of a serious tension between past and present was emphasized by Paul who, only 21-25 years after Jesus' death, acknowledged that the message about Jesus' cross must have seemed to be a *skandalon,* "a stumbling block to Jews and foolishness to Gentiles." [4] The scandal for much of subsequent theology has been the candor of Paul's primitive assessment:

"What could he, though so close to the action, have known that we do not know better?"

Religious Jews such as Peter and Paul knew exactly what the stumbling block was. It was not merely the controversial character of Jesus' life. That had been remarkably similar to the careers of prophets before him. The problem was the crucifixion.

Why was that an issue? Jewish piety had rested on the central teaching of the Torah. Moses' sermon in Deuteronomy, a rich exposition of the meaning of the Exodus and the Covenant that YHWH had established with Israel, revealed their identity as well as his own. The Covenant was a *berith,* a promise and obligation binding YHWH and his people to live henceforth in mutual fidelity, justice and love. The righteousness of Israel would result in a life of security, prosperity, and well being. This perspective, developed subsequently into a religious philosophy of history, dominates the Deuternomic tradition as set forth in six more books: Joshua, Judges, I and II Samuel, I and II Kings. Perhaps it is expressed most tellingly in those haunting lines that come as the climax in the first song in Israel's hymnbook. Countless millions of Jewish and Christian children have memorized it and have come to regard it as the guide for living a live of virtue.

> **Blessed is the man who walketh not in the counsel of the ungodly...**
> **But his delight is in the law of the LORD**
> **And on his law doth he meditate day and night...**
> **The ungodly are not so;**
> **But are like the chaff which the wind driveth away.**
> **Therefore the ungodly shall not stand in the judgment.**
> **Nor sinners in the congregation of the righteous.**
> **But the LORD knoweth the way of the righteous;**
> **But the way of the ungodly shall perish.** [5]

Blessed indeed are children who are lovingly taught this. But as they grow in years, they may notice that life does not quite work out that way for all good people, nor, in particular, did it seem to for Jesus. Was his crucifixion then evidence that he was among or even was ungodly? How could that be good news?

The classic theological/ethical problem, "why is life so unjust if God is truly sovereign?" is not dodged by the Hebrew Scriptures. Prophetic and learned texts address it in various ways. It is the central theme of the Book of Job, the paramount literary masterpiece of (1) Psalm 1:4-6 in the incomparable King James Version of the Hebrew Bible. [6] True, Job deploys much insight in its support of the Deuternomic tradition, but the drama as whole does not. Its brilliant climax actually deflects attention away from the core issue it had previously raised. Perhaps the wisdom traditions, ancient and modern, can do no better.

Nevertheless, the doctrine continues to have great power in both religion and culture. Everything from pedagogy to murder mysteries to partisan politics agree. Of course, we say, virtue pays and unrighteousness punishes. Of course virtue is the basis of prosperity and contentment. Of course injustice is destructive to the community and is usually personally self-destructive as well. The central truth of the perspective exemplified by Deuteronomy even seems convincing to many secular people—with or without the operation of God. It's vividly dominant in the doctrine of *karma of* Hinduism and its daughter religions as well: Virtue pays, unrighteousness punishes.

However, its weaknesses are apparent too, as some of Israel's psalmists and prophets first began to see. Its problems are not philosophical abstractions nor fictional speculations. The problems are ethical, universal, existential and, in at least in the case of the Hebrew Scriptures, rise directly from a religious understanding of what living justly means.

Let's listen to two voices. Amos and the poet commonly called Second Isaiah powerfully expanded the meanings of Israel's Deuternomic tradition in very different ways. The first of the so-called writing prophets, Amos (783-741 BCE) found a new assessment of the Deuternomic tradition. Nonetheless, even today it continues to have great power in both religion and culture. Everything from pedagogy to politics gets involved. Of course, we say, justice is the basis of prosperity and contentment. Of course injustice is destructive to the community and personally self-destructive as well. The basic truth of the perspective exemplified by Deuteronomy seems convincing to people cross culturally. But its weaknesses are apparent too, as some of Israel's psalmists and prophets began to see. Those problems are not abstract nor speculative. They are ethical, existential, and rise directly from the tradition's own understanding of its faith.

Amos and the poet commonly called Second Isaiah powerfully expanded in very different ways the tradition's potential. The first of the so-called writing prophets, Amos (783-741 BCE) found a new relevance in the Deuternomic message for the religion of his time. Citing a mass of evidence, [7] he employed breath-taking rhetoric in protesting that Israel' leaders had subverted the Covenant message of YHWH's redemption of Israel from bondage. They did this by suspending its ethical authority. He charged that they had acted as though there is no need for them to show gratitude for God's past mercy for Israel by working to build a community of justice now. Injustice will lead to punishment. Here's how Amos put it:

> **Thus says YHWH**
> **For three transgressions of Israel . . .**
> **I will not revoke the punishment**
> **Because they sell the righteous for silver.**
> **And the needy for a pair of sandals—**
> **They who trample the head of the poor into the dust of the earth**
> **And push the afflicted out of the way . . .**
>
> **For three transgressions of Judah . . .**
> **I will not revoke the punishment . . .**
> **Because they have rejected the law of YHWH**
> **And have not kept his statutes . .**
> **So I will send a fire on Judah**
> **And it shall devour the strongholds of Jerusalem. . . .**
>
> **Hear this word that YHWH has spoken against you,**
> **O people of Israel,**
> **against the whole family**
> **that I brought up out of the land of Egypt . .**

**I will punish Israel for its transgressions  
Prepare to meet your God, O Israel.** [8]

Years later, when North Israel and Judah had been defeated by their enemies, it seemed that Amos' cry clearly had been validated. His outrage was remembered and ultimately honored. Had he not shown that injustice does have consequences? His passion for justice was a rare gift. YHWH was speaking through him after all. Treasure his shocking words; they should be in the Bible, right next to Moses' Torah.

Amos also challenged Israel in a second way. This was his criticism of how Israel's chauvinism had abused its covenant with God. Israel's poor record ethically was connected to its superior attitude toward other peoples. In spite of Amos' self-mocking claim to be just a farm boy from the hill country down south, his remarkable knowledge of the cultural geography of the time amply demonstrates the breadth of his learning. It was intolerable that Israel's sense of identity should have become captive to a proud, self-serving tribalism. Surely YHWH, the creator of all people, is as concerned about other nations as he has shown himself to be for Israel. Speaking for YHWH again, he cried:

**Are you not like the Ethiopians to me?  
O people of Israel, says YHWH.**

**Did I not bring Israel up from the land of Egypt  
And the Philistines up from Caphtor  
And the Arameans up from Kir?** [9]

Early in the book Amos had insisted in graphic detail that YHWH demands justice from all peoples, Judah and North Israel not excepted. And now he shows YHWH to be the Shepherd of all other peoples as well. Amos does not say how the nations could possibly know or believe that. He probably assumed that YHWH would find a way.

Some two centuries after Amos, an unnamed prophet was sure that Amos' message of YHHW's punishment of Israel would not be the last word. The new word would be good news. He bravely announced that Israel's exile would surely end soon. Cyrus, the ruler of neighboring Persia and Babylon's old enemy, will come and triumph over the Babylonians. A second exodus awaits Israel. This astonishing message is preserved in the Book of Isaiah, chapters 40-55 (i.e. Second Isaiah). Imbedded within it are four puzzling poems, commonly called Servant Songs. [10] There is no consensus as to how these poems relate to Second Isaiah as a whole. For that matter, who is the servant? Is he an historical figure from the past, a contemporary figure, someone yet to come? Does he represent Israel in whole or in part? Perhaps poets then as now don't have to nail everything down. Ambiguity is the price of adventure.

Whatever the answer to these questions, it is important here to note the way these songs address Israel's problem with the Deuternomic tradition. The last song is a poignant picture of the suffering servant of YHWH called "See, my servant shall prosper."

> **The servant has been
> despised and rejected by others,
> a man of suffering and acquainted with infirmity.
> And as one from others hide their faces
> he was despised, and we held him of no account.**
>
> **Surely he has borne our infirmities
> and carried our diseases.
> Yet we accounted him striken,
> struck down by God, and afflicted.
> But he was wounded for our transgressions,
> crushed for our iniquities.
> Upon him was the punishment that made us whole
> and by his bruises we are healed.**
>
> **All we like sheep have gone astray
> We have all turned to our own way
> And YHWH has laid on him the iniquity of us all.** [11]

How would the exiles have understood the meanings of the Servant Songs? Would they have recognized themselves as the servant in these pictures? Do the pictures credibly reflect the life they had experienced? Or should they, like Amos' internationalist perspective, be considered signs of expectation?

Second Isaiah's take on the Deuternomic problem turned out to be good news in a couple of ways. One, certainly, was the fulfillment of a promise to Israel for a return from what today we call Iraq. The punishment for bad behavior is over. The debt has been paid. The captives can go free. The other bit of good news would take more time. Like some strange holiday rocket it would have to rotate upwards-- out of sight—soaring, soaring, waiting, waiting for a suitable time to explode.

It's easy to see that prophets like Amos and Second Isaiah had moved more deeply into an understanding of justice than had been previously thought possible. For example:

- *God's justice judges nations, not just individuals. Those to whom more is given, more is required.*
- *Law in Israel cannot be trivialized by being reduced to undemanding legalisms.*
- *Law is a demand for justice in all relationships with others and with God*
- *YHWH is the Shepherd of all peoples (Africa, Europe, Asia for starters)*
- *The suffering of the innocent is not their punishment. In a crisis it can be a power for making sinners aware, healed, free, whole.*
- *The world is unjust, but the faithful servant of YHWH is strong enough to challenge humanity by shouldering its iniquity and so transforming it.*

These prophetic voices did not have a political agenda although they could become politically subversive. They did not seek to establish a new religion; they sought to cleanse and expand what

God's justice had been believed to be. These voices proved to be irresistible for many and, of course, dangerous.

After years of neglect, this spirit of cleansing resurfaced in the career of John the Baptist. And then, very quickly, it flared out in the ministry of his northern cousin, Jesus of Nazareth. In this case the message centered specifically in the good news of yet another exodus. This time, it was claimed, the reign of YHWH would come to establish a new kind of sovereignty. Its vivid sign is a man who heals the sick, eats with sinners, feeds the hungry, embraces all sorts of outsiders like women (pious and not quite so pious), Samaritans, Gentiles and Roman soldiers. He boldly criticizes the religious establishment (lay and clergy) and then goes up to Jerusalem to proclaim there the coming of this new reign of YHWH. Of course Jerusalem had been prepared for his coming. Within five days it had managed to charge, prosecute, and kill him.

Years later, devout Muslims would say they cannot believe that God would permit this to happen to Jesus. He could not have been crucified. That would have been an act of God's unfaithfulness to a righteous prophet. God would have had to treat him as he did Elijah. Jesus too must have been permitted to ascend directly to heaven. He too would have been enabled to by-pass death.

But Jesus' own contemporaries did not say that. They said he really was crucified by the Romans. That testimony would prove literally crucial. The oldest Gospel had spoken frankly of his death. It also emphasized how frightened his best friends were. When three women went to the tomb as soon as they could to begin to prepare his abused body for ritual burial, they were astonished to find a young man sitting there. He tried but failed to reassure them by saying that "Jesus has been raised. He is not here." The women *were* alarmed and "fled from the tomb, for terror and amazement had seized them, and they said nothing to anyone for they were afraid." [12] Matthew, using another source, partly agrees and partly expands Mark's account saying that the women "left the tomb quickly with fear and great joy, and ran quickly to tell the disciples. Suddenly Jesus met them and said, 'Peace.' And they came to him, took hold of him by his feet, and worshiped him." [13]

It's surprising that while the sources the four Gospels depend on have much in common in their accounts of the last week of Jesus' life, they diverge significantly in their Easter narratives. Many years later, when the Gospels were gathered to form the first part of the New Testament, it is notable that there was no effort made to suppress these differences. The community must have thought that the variations didn't matter much. What did matter was the oral testimony they had heard right at the beginning, long before there had been any texts:

> **YHWH has raised Jesus from the dead.**
> **YHWH is stronger than death.**
> **Our crucified Messiah is with us still.**

It is particularly important to note that the earliest tradition preferred to speak of the resurrection not as a human triumph but as the action of the God of Israel:

> **This man...God raised up**
> **having freed him from death**
> **because it was impossible**
> **for him to be held in its power.** [14]

God is still at work. That is the claim. To make that affirmation credible, New Testament authors made heavy use of citations from the Hebrew Scriptures. These verses were understood to have anticipated this new demonstration of YHWH's characteristic coupling of sovereignty with intimacy, of holiness with presence. Nothing could have been more conventional than the freedom implicit in this method of God-centered reflection. The rabbinical tradition had been its nursery. Jesus himself no less than Paul would have taken it for granted. All that is needed then is to ask whether or not the prophet from Galilee, so charismatic, extraordinary and controversial was actually "the man whom God raised up," the man who therefore would be the promised Messiah of Israel, and thus the inheritor of all sorts of cognate biblical titles. Or not.

Since the central figure in the Gospels and all of his immediate followers were daughters and sons of Second Temple Judaism, the only answer that they would have found persuasive would have had to give primary attention to traditional biblical texts. Two issues are paramount.

First: Is the crucifixion of Jesus a sign of his having been rejected by God or not? The issue was not just whether he had been crucified; it was the claim that such a death could be God's work. From the perspective of Roman politics, God had nothing to do with it: The point of a crucifixion was political. It was intended to inflict dishonor on trouble makers' reputations and to terrify their followers into fearful submission. Such acts of public humiliation especially when fatal, had also been abhorrent to Israel's Deuteronomic lawmakers who decreed that a dead man "hung on a tree is under God's curse." [15]

But then, on the other hand, there were Jesus, his companions, and their friends who, could not have been totally unfamiliar with readings from Second Isaiah in the synagogue. Had the mysterious poet of the exile not explored religious meanings of what it would be like to be a suffering servant of YHWH? Had that strange portrait, roughly sketched centuries earlier, only now found its expected model? If the poet of the exile truly saw that YHWH could lay on the servant's back the iniquities of us all, then the suffering of the innocent could begin to be understood. God could use Rome's appalling brutality to achieve purposes that Rome had not intended, purposes which one day would subdue Rome —and empires far greater. Sovereignty could mean overcoming the strength of the strong by the weakness of the weak. [16] To be a man of sorrows, acquainted with grief, might mean the price it would take when one chooses to make intercession for transgressors who really do deserve to be punished. Until now this poetry may have seemed like a kind of unethical madness. But now it begins to become clearer that being regarded of no account may well be the price a herald will have to pay if news of liberation is to be brought to the captives. It's the price, they say, of doing business.

Only twenty years after the crucifixion, congregations were beginning to sing a new servant song. In one of his letters, Paul quotes a particularly well-crafted example of their art. An unknown poet had adopted the older servant songs as a model for an update that would clearly cite Jesus. It's also likely that he knew the similar humiliation-exaltation pattern in Psalm 21 since the Gospels had said that Jesus had prayed that as he hung on the cross. In both instances the dependence on Hebrew poetry in this so-called "Christ Hymn" is obvious. The song probably also antedates all four Gospels. It begins on a note of humiliation.

> **Though he was in the form of God**
> **he did not regard equality with God**
> **as something to be exploited,**
> **but emptied himself**
> **taking the form of a slave**
> **being born in human likeness.**
> **And being found in human form**
> **he humbled himself**
> **and became obedient unto the point of death—**
> **even death on a cross.**
>
> **Therefore God also highly exalted him**
> **and gave him the name**
> **that is above every name**
> **so that at the name of Jesus**
> **every knee should bend**
> **in heaven and on earth and under the earth**
> **and every tongue should confess**
> **that Jesus Christ is Lord.,**
> **to the glory of God the Father.** [17]

It would take a very long book, indeed, to unpack the significance of this poem. But we may note in passing just these seven items: (a) Its style and provenance shows it to be a very early Christian hymn. It is not a theological argument. (b) This poem was cited by Paul because of its practical relevance for ethics. (c) Its Christology is not the consequence of earlier work by Paul or John but is presupposed by them. (d) The poem dramatically connects Jesus' humiliation with his exaltation, sorrow with glory. (e) This coupling of humiliation and exaltation assumes YHWH's sovereignty, i.e. Hebrew monotheism. (f) In this tradition "the name above every name" would have to be YHWH. (g) Does "the form of God" mean "the identity of God" or "the image of God?" [18] Or both?

The New Testament almost always cites the Hebrew Bible as the authority for its truth claims. [19] This, of course, is the traditional rabbinical method and was essential for religious study in first century Judaism. Neither the authors of the New Testament texts nor the individuals they describe approached the Scriptures using methods familiar to modern students. [20] The task of the New Testament authors, all of whom except Luke were Jews, was simple. They straightforwardly sought to bring Israel's texts into connection with their experience of the gospel of the crucified and risen Lord.

Because of their emphasis on Israel's Scriptures, the early Jewish-Christian writers found it possible to bring them, as Richard Bauchham has pointed out "into relationship with the history of Jesus in a process of mutual interpretation from which their profoundest insights would come." [21]

Thus it was not the early Christians who had to resolve the old problem of how God could be involved in the suffering of the righteous. Second Isaiah had anticipated the problem and had offered creative theological options. Who would come and develop them? [22]

Second Isaiah had also addressed the problem that had troubled Amos earlier. In the eighth century BCE, Amos had charged that Israel's election does not mean YHWH's indifference to the plight of other nations. Israel is actually a typical case, a global exemplar of the mercy of God. Second Isaiah as well as Amos hears YHWH address all nations:

> **Turn to me and be saved, all the ends of the earth ...**
> **To me very knee shall bow, every tongue shall swear.** [23]

At first hesitatingly, and then increasingly, the Jesus movement began to face a second difficult challenge arising from the Hebrew texts, one even more problematic than the claim that a crucified rabbi had been raised from death by YHWH and had been given a new body. Surely that message could have only limited appeal to people who did not even know who YHWH was or meant. Again, however, the Hebrew Scriptures were seen by Jewish Christians to provide the rationale and the authority, if not the financing, for Israel's global mission. Its pioneer was, of course, Paul. By far the most sustained example of the depth of his commitment to a gospel for all people is set forth in his letter of self-introduction to the significant Jewish-Christian community in Rome. . Packed with dense theology, his apologetic turned out to be the most influential letter in the history of the world. Its arguments are still being debated by scholars--friend and foe. But its burden is simple. Paul needs to provide a rationale for his participation in Israel's vision of YHWH'S future:

**Turn to me and be saved
All the ends of the earth** [24]

The theological problem that strikes many modern readers of the New Testament seems not to have been a problem for its writers at all. We call it monotheism. If Jesus is the Son of God, something that the New Testament does not question, does that not obscure, if not repudiate, monotheism? Ever since the eighteenth century, writers have claimed that the early Christians misunderstood Jesus when they mistakenly turned him into a god deserving of divine honors. "It's our job today to correct them since we today certainly understand the past better than they who were its participants could possibly have been able to do" is the dogmatic assumption. Be that as it may, it is striking that a community whose basic authority was the Hebrew scriptures saw Jesus' identity not only as being human but just as obviously as something more than that. What was that something more? Why did no one then seem to think that whatever name we give it, they did not speak of a second god at all. It is YHWH acting afresh but with characteristic freedom and justice and mercy to redeem Israel and all people.

Baukham has shown how "early Christians included Jesus, precisely and unambiguously, within the unique identity of the one God of Israel." [25] The monotheism of Second Temple Judaism in the first century was strict: God is clearly distinguished from all creatures including angels and priests and natural phenomena. The Scripture's references to God's creating the world through his word and wisdom is not a threat to monotheism but a figurative way of referring to God's sovereign action in creation and history. It is Israel's characteristic way of stressing YHWH's unique identity. [26] The ancient world was, of course, full of gods. Even Caesar could qualify. That YHWH is not just one of a class but is incomparable was beyond question in Second Temple Judaism. The diverse and expressive ways in which the Scriptures express YHWH's identity was not an embarrassment, it is Judaism's most glorious achievement.

What does this have to do with Jesus? Why, in particular, did the New Testament's authors take it for granted that he was Israel's Messiah and Son of God, if that meant they all would have had to agree to abandon belief in YHWH's unique identity? Their reading of the Scriptures made that unacceptable move unnecessary.

Here are a few examples:

Psalm 110:1 is referred to directly or indirectly twenty-one times by these Jewish Christians, "YHWH said to my Lord, 'Sit at my right hand, until I make your enemies your footstool.'" Why this frequency? Non-Christian Jews rarely cited Psalm 110. The early Christians understood the Lord being addressed to be Jesus. There is no evidence that they as Jews saw this as a threat to YHWH'S unique sovereignty and identity. God's raising of Jesus at Easter was his exaltation of him, a coronation celebrating his messiahship now understood to be a sharing in YHWH'S sovereignty over all things.

Ephesians 1:21-22 echoes the Christ Hymn in Philippians. It declares that God, having raised Jesus from the dead, has placed him above the angels and has given him "the name that is above every name...and has put all things under his feet." The bestowal of that name as well as a participation in the creation of all worlds is announced at the beginning of the Letter to the Hebrews (1:1-4) in yet another effort to connect the Hebrew Scriptures to the passion and resurrection of Jesus.

A consensus can be discerned in this tradition of reading the Scriptures:

Neither the death nor the resurrection of Jesus is in conflict with the sovereign identity of the God of Israel. To the contrary, they validate and demonstrate it. YHWH, who is enduringly faithful, has spoken in Jesus' work of self-giving as his own word of reconciliation for the whole world. That gift of peace now shines in all creation through Jesus who, like all of us, is made in the image of YHWH and who unlike any of us is now present universally showing forth YHWH's own identity.

What are we to make of all this?

Modernity often pictures God as impotent if not absent altogether. Israel's prophets said much the same about the idols popular in their time. It all depends on what one assumes the word God to mean. Whatever one thinks of the witness of the first Christians, a feckless God does not seem quite to fit what they were talking about. Maybe the problem is that modernity so often accepts impotence as the fair price for avoiding intimacy.

Literary critics have often pointed out that contemporary writers generally prefer to see human life in tragic terms. Some, but not all, of the ancient Greeks would have agreed. However, the biblical gospel in both Testaments does not and thus is deeply subversive of the modern sensibility. Sorrow and suffering and death, key elements in the tragic view of life, are by no means absent in the Bible. In fact they are set forth so strongly that some find the Bible offensive on that account alone. Nonetheless, nothing could be clearer than that a narrative that ends with a resurrection, the triumph of life, light and love, can not possibly be called tragic. Perhaps, for some of us, it is this option for hope that is offensive. The coming of a life of love and hope could change everything we have been counting on.

The belief that Jesus was both crucified and risen made it possible, actually inevitable, that he would be designated Messiah (or Christ)--titles that are sparingly used in the Gospels and which typically occasion confusion. He was not the Messiah if that meant he was simply another David, a soldier, a national hero for a particular group of tribes. But if events can reshape language, then a new, if controversial, meaning may become inevitable. Other titles for Jesus invite reflection. Jesus appears to have preferred the title "Son of Man," but the church has been reluctant to follow him in this. The title is idiomatic, not literal, and has two seemingly different meanings (a) Humanity , as in Psalm 8, and (b) YHWH's agent (individual or corporate) that comes at the end of time to establish God's just rule over all nations, as in Daniel 7. The two meanings need not be contradictory, but Jesus seems to have preferred the second which strongly implies divine agency. The title "Son of God" early became very popular in the Gentile world where it had commonly been used to refer to kings and persons of power. In the church this title has come to be virtually synonymous with the title "Christ or Messiah." Messiah refers to a prophet, priest, or king in Israel who was the one anointed (in Greek, *Christos*) to serve God. Since all the titles are symbolic and easily misunderstood, care should be taken not to obscure the testimony that the title "Christ" refers to a unique servant who was crucified and rose again, i.e. a crucified Messiah.

## CHAPTER SIX

# From Moses to Martin

Judaism and Christianity are in fundamental agreement concerning ethics and spirituality.

This consensus should not be a surprise to anyone:

*(a) They agree that spirituality and ethics are inseparable.*
*(b) They agree that this connection is grounded in God's identity, his saving presence in all he has made.*
*(c) The connection is insuperable.*

The only problem is the importance which each tradition is willing to assign to what they claim to be fundamental. Their hesitation is easy to understand even if it is difficult to defend. The strategy of this chapter will not attempt to do that. Our task is to free this insuperable agreement from its ugly mantle, a kudzu of envy and blame.

Where did this consensus come from? According to the classic sources, it is grounded in a cluster of events that occurred in Arabia and northeast Africa about 1290 BCE. An Israelite with an Egyptian name led a revolt against Pharaoh Rameses II by gathering a group of slaves in an exodus out of Egypt to the edge of Canaan. The religious meaning of this act of liberation was Moses' breakthrough to a new understanding of the nature of God. God's new name is YHWH which can be translated as "I am who I am," "I am what I am," or "I will cause to be." [1] God as YHWH has heard the cry of this oppressed people and, through Moses, will act to bring them out of bondage to freedom. Holiness is understood to be active in history as a transcendent yet personal intervention of justice and mercy for a downtrodden people.

The presence and purposes of YHWH can be deeply subversive. They contrast starkly to the emphasis on stability, permanence, and changelessness characteristic of Egypt's gods. What enabled Moses to make his breakthrough? How was it possible for the God of the patriarchs be seen now as the champion, the savior, of the oppressed? Perhaps it had been there all the time. Perhaps not. Perhaps the modern reluctance of many to commit themselves to a connection between spirituality and ethics is related to something else they share: a lack of appreciation for the transformative power of Moses' vision. [2]

The connection is certainly clear in the *Shema*, repeated each day by the faithful for over three thousand years:

> **Hear, O Israel,**
> **YHWH is our God,**
> **YHWH alone.**
> **You shall love YHWH, your God,**
> **with all your heart,**
> **and with all our soul,**
> **and with all your might.** [3]

This is not a prayer. It is a command to a community. It exactly defines the required response for having been freed from bondage. Note a few of its features:

- *The command, Shema, is decisive: "Hear me." He who is "I am who I am" is not a dumb idol, passively waiting for a worshipper to come and offer a gift. He is the holiness of all that is--now demanding silence, inviting listening: Listen to what you need to hear if you are to be connected to the giver of all life, the author of your being, the designer of your being well. The whole community is called to attention. Is anyone willing to listen?*

- *Equally significant is the triple rhythm of the divine name echoed in the triple responses of human love. This name is holy. It is so holy that some are reluctant to say it out loud. But without a name or its circumlocution, how can one identify what/who it is that displayed the connection between holiness and justice? Between holiness and freedom? And now, repeatedly, between holiness and human love? Did this connection come from the gods of Egypt acting in concert? Or is it, as some want to claim, self-evident? Or did it come from nothing at all so that it is ultimately-- nothing at all? The Shema denies all this; it declares repeatedly that human love is rooted in holiness and that holiness is present in human life.*

- *"Alone" means more than "one." "Alone" is not a rationally obvious mathematical abstraction. "Alone" means "exclusive loyalty" or "consistent faithfulness." The beautiful and treasured King James version's translation of this verse in Deuteronomy 6:4 is anachronistic and inadequate.*

- *For most modern readers, "love" is the most problematic word in the Shema. Ever since Freud, love has mostly been understood to be the romantic word for libido, that intense sexual desire that drives all forms of animal life. Moses was not unaware of its power. He probably knew what the prophets after him knew: sexual desire was a basic element in the old religions of Canaan. For the Shema love is not the ancient preoccupation with a natural biological force: relentless, sweaty, polymorphous, perverse. Love meant basically an exclusive connection.*

- *"Heart" did not mean what it means in modern biology or poetry. The heart was understood to be the seat of thinking and willing, i.e. the mind, not emotion or feeling.* [4] *"Might" means power—the very word the conventionally religious often say they fear.*

The insuperable agreement is repeated and stressed in the three Synoptic Gospels. It is significant, however, that they report that the rabbi from Nazareth altered and expanded the traditional account. He performed a bit of surgery by inserting a fragment from Leviticus (the Mt. Sinai version) into the classic Mt. Horeb narrative given in Deuteronomy:

**You shall love your neighbor as yourself.** [5]

Why did he do this? Isn't this a tampering with a supposedly verbally inspired sacred text? Jesus' grafting the Leviticus verse into Deuteronomy's makes it immediately clear that the object of the law of God is not only God himself, but one's neighbor, potentially all of humankind. This surgery makes it explicit that the command to love God unconditionally is connected to a social obligation: care for your neighbor as much as you care for your self. Taken legalistically both commands are impossible to obey. Understood as rooted in a spirituality, both commands dramatically expand ordinary assumptions about human moral and mystical competence. The elevation of the obligation to deal with all other human beings lovingly moves far beyond the universal Golden Rule which, of course, does no such thing.

John's Gospel, as usual, raises the stakes higher. Rather than combining the two texts from the Torah, Jesus here places human moral/spiritual life on a different foundation. At 15:12 he presents a new exemplar, a new expectation, apparently a new empowerment:

**This is my commandment,
that you love one another
as I have loved you.
No one has greater love than this,
To lay down one's life for one's friends.** [6]

And yet, he is still well within the orbit of the *Shema*. The holy in human experience remains within the *Shema's* scope of self giving—mentally, comprehensively, and powerfully.

Two other considerations need attention. First: Is it appropriate to speak of holiness in personal terms?

The Hebrew and Greek Testaments use both personal and impersonal language to speak of the holy. That is not a contradiction since it is not possible to understand adequately even human life without using both personal and impersonal language, i.e. an awareness of self-consciousness in terms of one's uniqueness and having access to the generalizations of the social and biological science respectively. If our sense of what is ultimate can be expressed in personal terms, our ultimate loyalties will be personally significant. If we can only trust the generalizations of the sciences, a sense of personal significance disappears. To know broadly what being human means requires having the ability to have access to both languages.

The biblical writers freely used richly personal language in speaking of the action of the holy. Abraham spoke directly to God as a personal friend. [7] At Mt. Horeb's burning bush, it was not the fire, it was a personal voice that challenged Moses to go back to Egypt and lead the slaves to freedom. Are these foundational texts too primitive to be taken seriously? Or is it that modern readers need to try to learn how to read ancient texts?

The other problem is not literary but ethical. It lies in our confusions about the meanings of justice. What child, no matter how well protected, does not learn that life isn't fair? Why should one expect otherwise? Do we have to toughen them up, turn our children into precocious Stoics, to save them from getting hurt? "Just lower your sights, Buster, and you'll be OK?" Or is it not rather that being human includes an expectation that being treated fairly and being fair oneself is the price of admission to the so-called human race? Don't even some animals have some sense of this?

If your friend is not fair to you, you may need to get a new friend. Or, at least, try to find out what's the problem. Paying no attention is a very bad idea. Being fair and being treated fairly are universally regarded as indispensable and are the basic assumption of all ethical life. It is not surprising then that in the ancient Middle East, Hebrew texts made prominent use of such words as *tsedeq* and *mispat*. usually translated as righteousness and justice.[8] Being fair, being just, seeking and demanding justice from oneself and others was the immediate measure of holiness. To be holy is to be just.

Three crises in Israel's life affirmed and enlarged that assumption.

(a) *The exodus experience was definitive. Moses at Horeb and Hosea in North Israel spoke of the exodus as an act of justice inspired by the loving-kindness (hesid) of YHWH. Mercy demands justice. Justice affirms rights and responsibilities. Mercy springs from compassion and love. In YHWH there is no conflict between steadfast love and righteousness  They are not abstractions that reside on a mental shelf in an ideal world. They are the living tissue of human life—corporate and personal. The blood of the moral life flows through them. They are a central part of what it means to be created in the image of God.*

(b) *The exile was the second crisis. Why did Israel lose its Temple and its land? Amos said it was because justice required God to punish an unjust people. That judgment, grim though it be, at least made the exile intelligible. But Second Isaiah objected: We have had to suffer twice as much as we deserved, he protested. The problem here is inescapable. A traditional belief held that divine justice is a matter of rewards and punishments. So claiming that God rewards the righteous and punishes the wicked does not explain why innocent people have to suffer. Either God has forgotten us or something new has happened. What could that be?*

*Suppose an innocent servant of God suffers unjustly. Why does God permit that? The servant is not being punished for what he has done. Rather, he is picking up an obligation that is not rightfully his own. If he does this freely, willingly, that would require a change in the meaning of justice. It could now mean an exchange that would move beyond retaliation. An unjust person had received a transformative gift she did not deserve. She could now be freed, healed for a new life. This redaction of an ancient understanding of justice was not a Christian invention.*

(c) *The third crisis in Israel was the crucifixion of Jesus. The catastrophe of Jesus' death had stunned his followers. His mission had obviously failed. He really had been killed like a common criminal. But then the disciples, men and the women were astounded again. In spite of their doubt and fears, YHWH had proven trustworthy. He had exalted Jesus by giving him a new kind of life, a new form, a new body. They remembered that when Jesus had prayed Psalm 22 on the cross, he had to know that it began in anguish and ended in triumph. Once again YHWH had proven not to be impotent, unjust, unloving. The resurrection of Jesus was a vindication of YHWH's justice quite as much as an exaltation of the crucified Messiah. This is what the disciples after Easter dared proclaim publically.*

The resurrection moves Israel's understanding of justice to a new level. The death of a new servant of God rendered the old notion of death as punishment for unrighteousness could make no sense in this case. If death cannot be rationalized as punishment, what is it? The singer of the Song of Solomon knew that the love of lovers is stronger than death. That is deeply true and far from obvious. So, if justice is more than an agent of punishment, what can it be?

It is more than punishment when it is seen as an agent of mercy. Justice itself is redeemed when "what is right" is seen as inclusive of the whole adventure of humanity. Justice is far more than a legal system of rewards and punishments. Justice is a life that is shaped by its own history. The past is strong but not strong enough to hold the creation in its grip forever. The present is powerful, but it is very fragile-- immediately swallowed by onrushing time. The discovery of the reality of the future—which of course does not exist in space and time--transcends all that we know, all that we can control. As it comes, full of surprises, it overpowers our understandings what has been. The resurrection shows that it can be the context for a redeemed justice.

So how is justice responsive to the future? The resurrection is a demonstration of the light and life coming to us from God's future. What will be is not what has been. What is is not what will be. This vision of movement is morally significant. While living fully requires having access to memory and being attentive to the present, it is above all being able to do this in the light of God's future. The image of God as lived by the Son of Man was an intimation of the human story from the perspective of God's future. In that future justice is not an agent of punishment. It is an affirmation of life shaped by transcendent, evocative love. It is what the New Testament calls the good news: humanity's journey from death to life.

Understanding the resurrection as a response to this third crisis has always been controversial—even within the Church. How can the acquittal of all those unrighteous people be consistent with, much less an enlargement of, the older belief that a righteous God is required to see to it that the unrighteous are punished? An influential party among the Christians living in Rome in the first century found this problematic. Paul knew they saw this as a problem. Perhaps it could also be an opportunity. Paul had been planning to go to Spain from Corinth by way of Rome. Why not write the Roman church about his travel plans? He could write a personal letter of introduction which could also serve to lay out a solution to their theological problems. He could show them how the message of the resurrection profoundly affects the meaning of

God's righteousness. Actually it is not only ethically possible for God to acquit sinners. The resurrection is God' supreme, cosmic act in a justice of reconciliation.

The first eight chapters of Paul's letter reads like the draft for a courtroom drama. [10] Paul seems to have been influenced by the Book of Job which had earlier used the same fictive venue for a different purpose. Paul had spent enough time in being hauled into court to have a vivid sense of how things work there. The judge, of course, represents God. The defendant is all humankind—Jews and Gentiles alike. The prosecution is the old justice system of punishments and rewards. The defense attorney is not Jesus. It is that audacious tent-maker, Paul, himself. Moderns usually find the narrative's style and method of argument off-putting, but it would have been familiar to rabbis in first century Rome.

The good news is that something has happened to enable God's justice to work in a new way. Israel and all people have a new champion, one who breaks down the barriers of hostility that have separated them from one another and from God.. That something is the death and resurrection of Christ. The crucifixion was a blatant, public demonstration of a demand for injustice. Major institutions of justice chose to destroy a just man, the Son of Man, the new Adam coming among us from God's future. The resurrection is God's protest against the agents of the public order so eager to be instruments of punishment. His protest is an affirmation, the intervention of a new creation, openly displayed in the exaltation of his Son. Justice can not be served by punishing the righteous. In the new creation even the unrighteous are not punished. They are acquitted by God. Jew and Gentile alike are enabled to enter this life of a new justice measured by salvation, freedom, regeneration, and hope. The resurrection enables us to see its cosmic scope. For Paul what is deeply personal is also cosmic in implication:

> **I consider that the sufferings of this present time are not worth comparing with the glory about to be revealed to us. For the creation waits with eager longing**

> for the revealing of the children of God. For the creation was subjected to futility (not of its own will but by the will of one who subjected it) in hope that the creation itself will be set free from its bondage to decay and will obtain the freedom of the glory of the children of God.
> We know that the whole creation has been groaning in labor pains until now. And not only creation, but we ourselves who have the first fruits of the Spirit, groan inwardly while we wait our adoption, the redemption of our bodies. For in hope we are saved. (11)

His rhapsody ends as it began on a deeply personal note.

> I am convinced that neither death, nor life
> nor angels, nor rulers,
> nor things present, nor things to come,
> nor powers, nor height nor depth,
> nor anything else in all creation,
> will be able to separate us from the love of God,
> in Christ Jesus our Lord. (12)

Paul's personal exploration of the powers of divine love to expand and transform justice has reverberated across cultures, across the world. In the West, Augustine, Abelard and Aquinas found it a major inspiration as the ancient world tottered toward its death. The reformers recaptured its importance for a Church which had forgotten how to repent. In the nineteenth century it escaped the prisons of Western culture and began to grow vigorously in Asia and Africa. And in the twentieth century creative theologians showed how it could remain decisive for biblical, ethical and philosophical reflection.

## Worldly Justice

In political thought, however, thinking about justice shifted to secular considerations. In the eighteenth century Enlightenment, attention was directed away from the cosmic and religious meanings of justice to its political and mundane aspects. The American experience at this point proved somewhat atypical in part because Americans, for the most part, did not see themselves as hostile to religion and in part because religion's capacity for moral stability was seen as an asset for building a society on law and order.

It is important to remember that long before the Enlightenment philosophers had begun their work, it was well understood by the churches, established and independent alike, that they had a double duty. They were responsible for the nurture and growth of the spiritual life of their communities. And they were responsible for the social well being of the public as a whole. Puritans in New England and Anglicans in Virginia took that double responsibility for granted however they might disagree with each other on doctrines of faith and order. Thus it was possible for the new nation's founding documents to appeal to the public role of religion without requiring any church to assume the burden of national establishment

The Declaration of Independence is the basic text. It fittingly reflects the spirit of its time by making a variety of references to the role of God in the founding of the new nation. He is Nature's God as well as the Creator of humanity to whom he has given numerous inalienable rights. He is also the Supreme Judge of the whole world and, most significantly in this context, Divine Providence, i.e. divinity understood as guiding and sustaining human destiny. Was this so much conventional boiler plate? As though they anticipated the cynic's suspicion, the signers claimed at the conclusion of their confession that to support it they pledged nothing less than their *sacred* honor. True, a deist among others could speak of "Nature's God." The other three designations for divinity, however, are unmistakably biblical. The bold claim is that the God they have in mind acts in nature and history to guide, judge and endow all people with such rights as life, liberty and the pursuit of happiness. This is not deism nor secularism. This is a remarkably sophisticated and skillful confession of political theology which neither contradicts nor identifies any local religious tradition. It is not boiler plate: it lay its writers open to the charge of treason. Centuries later the practical value of these self evident truths has proved increasingly attractive world-wide.

Whatever the excellence of the Declaration of 1776, the founders knew it would be impotent if it were to stand alone. What would be the structure that could obligate the new nation and its citizens to make the Declaration effective? Covenants had been the way in which ancient peoples transformed visions into political instruments. Without covenants, sacred contracts, visions can just float away--mere dreams of what might have been. In 1787, eleven years later, a Constitution of the United States was ratified by the Congress to provide the appropriate structure. The two documents form a coherent whole. The six goals for the new nation as set forth in the Constitution's Preamble neatly tie the newer text to its predecessor. When in 1791 a Bill of Rights was added, the first Amendment, significantly, addresses religion. There is a common belief today that the Constitution deals with religion by erecting "a wall of separation between Church and State." The phrase, however, is not constitutional. It was Thomas Jefferson's personal affirmation of what he correctly understood to be the theological view of Rhode Island Baptists when he sought to commend them. The Constitution itself has a different interest. It does not affirm Baptist polity nor does it establish secularism. What it does is more subtle and more pragmatic. It assesses the relation of the federal government to religion in the new nation. It neatly balances two principles--both of which are designed to restrict the power of the federal government.

First of all, the Congress may not "respect an establishment of religion." Churches and mosques established and recognized by national governments were common in the eighteenth century. In the twentieth century synagogues were added to the list. That would be illegal federally in the United States. Typically such establishments confer political and financial advantages but also compromise the integrity, autonomy, and freedom of religious communities and make them directly subject to political control. This restriction of congressional power is thus commonly seen to favor the freedom of religious communities.

Secondly, the Congress may not prohibit the free exercise of religion. Without this prohibition it would be possible for the government to prosecute religious communities for political reasons. If, however, the free exercise of religion contradicts other rights embedded in the Constitution, the free exercise would need to be qualified. In the nineteenth century it came to be claimed that biblical polygamy should be considered a part of the free exercise of religion and therefore should be legal in the United States. In the twentieth century it was determined that the government many not compel persons to salute the flag if they believe that practice to be forbidden by the Ten Commandments. Today the determination of what qualifications of the free exercise of religion are legal is very much a work in progress particularly in issues dealing with biomedical ethics. The point, however, is clear. The government does not have the power to require citizens to violate their religious beliefs. Both the left and the right find this restriction disturbing—if for opposite reasons.

At the birth of the nation it was repeatedly claimed that the liberty on which it was founded was nothing less than the gift of the Creator. To guard that freedom was a sacred duty. That liberty and justice was a God-given right intended for all was undoubted. Patriotic speeches on the Fourth of July and evangelical sermons on the first Sunday in July insisted on it. And yet, the realities could be very different. If liberty is God-given then how can it be that freedom is for many people an unattainable dream? If the nation was founding on the expectation of liberty and justice for all, why has that religious vision collapsed into fragments?

No nineteenth century American writer saw how fragile the connection between freedom and justice had become than did Mark Twain. The canonical text, "The Adventures of Huckleberry Finn,." reads like a comedy. [13] Huck and Jim, an escaped slave, are floating slowly down the Mississippi. Huck was troubled. He was grateful that Jim had saved his life, but he knew that it would be wrong to help Jim escape to freedom. There were penalties for lawbreakers. He remembered *"that people that acts as I'd been acting about that nigger goes to everlasting fire."*

The right thing to do was clear. His duty was to write to Jim's owner so he could reclaim his property. That would be tough. Huck wasn't much for praying, but he tries to pray for strength to do what he had been taught was right. But then that turned out to be the problem.

> I was trying to make my mouth say I would do the right thing and the clean thing, and go and write to that nigger's owner and tell where he was, but deep down inside I knowed it was a lie, and He knowed it. You can't pray a lie—I found that out . . .

In spite of what he'd been taught by Aunt Sally, Huck's conscience got in the way. What was he supposed to do? He just took up the letter

> ...and held it in my hand. I was trembling, because I'd got to decide,forever, betwixt two things, and I knowed it. I studied a minute, sort of holding my breath and then says to myself: All right then I'll *go* to hell—and tore it up.
> It was awful thoughts, and awful words, but they was said. And I let them stay said; and never thought no more about reforming.

A religiously informed culture had overriding economic reasons for determining that some people were not really a part of the Constitution's "We, the people." They were someone's property and that therefore the Creator had not given them inalienable rights to liberty and life. Huck knew that very well. He also knew that his conscience would not let him believe that. What you need is the strength to go against a conventionally religious community. You got to listen to the voice that tells you to act. You got to save Jim no matter what. So just do it. Huck'll never be able to please Aunt Sally anyhow.

The question for the reader who gets to be with Huck on the raft is, "What is Twain up to?" Is he condemning the religious culture of that time and place? Is he showing that liberty and justice for all is more than a bit of solemn rhetoric--they are a part of the inalienable right that the Declaration talks about? Is it his recognition that the moral life of untutored Huck is guided by a conscience that inexplicably enables even compels him to do what's right even if he has to go to hell for it? Or, is it all of this?

Huck used conscience to override Aunt Sally's religion. [14] What's conscience, this "knowing with" that enables us to hear words of justice, to exercise moral discernment, to act righteously? Unlike a potted plant but like others animals we are able to be conscious when we are awake. As we grow in years we are increasingly able to explore what it means to know that we know we know. Beyond this self-consciousness there is a third step. Conscience is the moral depth of consciousness. It means that we are able to judge, affirm and love what we are doing and thinking and hoping.. Conscience is the capacity to understand what it is to be judged, accepted and loved. Conscience is the moral capacity to listen and to be listened to. It is the opening to a personal connection to the midnight sky's display of a "beauty not our own." It is having access to the reality of truth beyond what we have understood to be true, to the presence of authentic goodness even though all our experience has been compromised by what is not good. It is an awareness that every person has a unique identity even though we cannot possibly know every person to know whether that could be true. It is the root of that strange sense of knowing what is not confined to our experience but to which we are bound nonetheless. It is something "closer to us than we are to ourselves." It is what is meant, in part, by the presence of the holy. Conscience is not a moral blank page. It has a history beyond our knowing even as it gives us the capacity to know that we are connected to all things. Huck knew much of this. Few, if any of us, know all of it.

A sick conscience can be very dangerous. It can drive a friend to suicide when self-judgment is wounded by shame, despair or guilt. It can drive a nation to war because of social fear, anger or greed. Contemporary fiction and films aggressively explore the consequences of our pervasive modern tragedy—the decay of conscience. But these aberrations are not inevitable. Conscience, personal and social, can be robust and healthy. Conscience can be the agent for our ability to accept that we have been accepted even when we are most reluctant to believe that. Conscience can enable us to transcend the injustices of life that attack us and those whom we love. Conscience is the hard wiring that makes forgiveness personally accessible. The reasonable test for all spiritualities is whether they challenge, embrace and nurture access to a healthy, life-affirming conscience.

What happens when conscience is in contact with the sacred human need to connect freedom with justice? What difference does it make for family life, for communities, and for the planet? What happens when our spiritualities are freed from their irresponsibility, their escape into privatism? What happens when a weak conscience severs the bond between rights and responsibilities?

As we have seen, the biblical visionaries had found a way to urge a more aggressive and creative understanding of justice than their cultures had permitted. Their success has often been ignored if not denied. But it has never been utterly forgotten. It is uncanny how at critical times in unexpected places it has reemerged. [15] In nineteenth century America, for example, it had become increasingly clear that the young nation no longer believed itself to be obliged to respect its founders' moral views. The prevailing understanding of the Constitution had commonly been permitted to override the basic affirmations of the Declaration. Whatever the founders' intent had been it was now clear that all men are not created equal, they are not endowed by their Creator with certain inalienable rights which include life, liberty and the pursuit of happiness. The Declaration's lengthy complaints against the King of Britain were trivial in comparison to the abuses of political justice perpetrated by the Americans against their own people.

Advocates for a return to the neglected values of the Enlightenment were few and went unheeded. But most people who could read did have in their homes at least one book which proved unexpectedly, dangerously relevant. The biblical prophets' passion for justice and freedom struck some as a judgment while for others it was a promise, the promise that mattered. Divine Providence is not through with this people just yet.

Even before Abraham Lincoln and the Civil War, a womanist theologian and social activist, Sojourner Truth, traveled "up and down the land" demanding justice for her people and for women generally. Oppression comes in many forms but it will surely be overcome by the goodness of God she promised.

The President offended many when he invited this female prophet to visit him in the White House. Why did he do that? He knew it was politically risky to treat a black woman with respect. But had he not headed down this path back there in Illinois in 1858? He had told the farmers in Alton what he thought about the enslavement of people by a nation that claimed to be built on devotion to liberty and justice. The dispute over slavery had many causes. But at its core it is a spiritual,

> **eternal struggle between two principles**
> **--right and wrong—**
> **throughout the world..**
> **It is the same spirit that says,**
> **"You toil and work and earn bread**
> **--and I'll eat it."**
> **No matter in what shape it comes,**
> **it is the same tyrannical principle.**

It is easy to dismiss rhetoric about eternal principles. But the principles turned out to be a simple matter of economic justice Every farmer could see that: Slavery is theft. How can that be all right?

Five years later in a small town in Pennsylvania, the President would prove more contemplative than he had been in Alton. The ghastly war was still grinding on. But now it was about much more than economics. He seems not to have forgotten Sojourner Truth and her luminous but utterly unsentimental belief in the goodness of God. But he dared to go further. Like a biblical prophet he wrestled for a meaning, actually a godly meaning, that could be found in the appalling carnage that this young nation, so bountifully blessed in so many ways, had now chosen to visit upon itself. Who could dare hope that any goodness of God could come out of this national fratricide, brothers killing brothers, en mass, endlessly? Is there anything we can hope for after all this? Is there anything that we can do?

Actually, there is. As we bury our sons and brothers in Gettysburg's lovely fields,

> **We here highly resolve**
> **that these dead shall not have died in vain;**
> **that this nation, under God,**
> **shall have a new birth of freedom;**
> **and that the government**
> **of the people**
> **by the people**
> **and for the people**
> **shall not perish from the earth.**

Seven years after his Sojourner Truth visit, in his Second Inaugural, he showed that his resolve at Gettysburg had not been in vain. He gave to the wounded nation a new charge, stronger, clearer and politically breathtaking:

**With malice toward none;
with charity for all;
with firmness in the right
as God gives us to see the right.
let us strive on to finish the work we are in;
to bind up the nation's wounds,
to care for him who shall have borne the battle,
and for his widow and his orphan,
to do all which may achieve and cherish
a just and a lasting peace
among ourselves and with all nations.**

America's Abraham had become an Amos and then a Paul. He believed that the war had been a punishment, a judgment of God on a nation heedless of its obligation to keep its own political and moral covenant, one witnessed to, they had claimed, by the Supreme Judge of the world. The founding documents were a solemn, sacred contract which the people had deliberately violated by enslaving people from distant Africa, and generations of their descendents. The war had been a sign of God's bitter but just judgment on the American people, a people grown indifferent to their own demands for justice and the obligations of liberty.

Yet, in the biblical tradition, justice is not only judgment against unrighteousness. Justice is also the work of mercy, that splendid firmness in the right as God gives us to see the right. Our constitutional obligation to provide for the general welfare can now be rightly focused on our caring for orphans and widows and wounded veterans. Our constitutional duty to strive for the blessings of liberty for ourselves and our posterity can now be rightly expanded so we can work to achieve a just and lasing peace among ourselves and with all nations in the world.

In significant measure Abraham Lincoln's reunited nation grew into his vision of a future of justice, liberty and peace. But major elements in that hope have yet to be realized. A just and lasting peace with all nations is as far off now as it ever has been. As for the nation's paying the bills for their enslavement of the Africans, that would be postponed to some unspecified future. In the meantime all would pay something and our Africans would continue to pay the most.

In our time a progressive African-American preacher dared believe that he was called by the Supreme Judge of the world to do something about the substance of Lincoln's vision. It was no problem for Martin Luther King to find voices in the Church's Testaments that were salient to the nation's struggle with injustice. It's all there: God bestows and requires justice and mercy and freedom for all people. Unfortunately, God's inclusivity is culturally offensive. Many people don't like this kind of talk one bit, and find ways, often violent, to stop the voices of those who echo it. But there are those, like Martin, while knowing that very well, are still willing to take the risk of having to pay the price which a moral transformation of the nation will require. Martin's rhetoric, biblical and beautiful, is a national treasure. But it is his life and death that is the greater witness. It is hard to find people who will give all they are to move the world to embrace the justice it needs for its healing. Martin was such a one. He did not believe in building walls that are dedicated to separate communities of faith from the structures of public justice. He believed in engagement and encounter. He had the courage to believe that the ancient and future justice of God is at work now judging and recreating humankind. He had the courage to believe that ordinary people could be a part of that. That was his dream. [16]

## CHAPTER SEVEN

## On Being Well and Being Well- Connected

America's constitutional intent to become a more perfect union has been very much a work in progress. The previous chapter sketched ways in which the public has struggled over time to realize the power of its originating dream of liberty and justice for all. The role of its religious communities in defining their vocation in this project has been puzzling and controversial--both internally and publically. It has also been more fruitful than any of the nation's founders could have imagined.

The present chapter briefly reviews some of the ways in which the churches have come to be advocates for public justice. This has been, and still is, deeply controversial. People ask: Does not adopting a public role compromise a religion's integrity? Does not love of country require religious institutions to support the political establishment? Is there not a danger that a religious community may become so engaged with its public role that it may lose its soul?

These are not new questions at all. They are much older than the American republic. They have, however, come to be addressed with special vigor in modern times. The witness of Martin Luther King is an example. He seemed extraordinary to his contemporaries within and outside the churches. But he did not think so. He freely acknowledged his indebtedness to a broadly inclusive tradition. The non-violent spirituality of the Hindu, Mahatma Gandhi, the optimistic social gospel of Walter Rauschenbusch, and its maturation in the bracing realism of Reinhold Niebuhr all proved decisive for him. This Protestant effort to identify the churches' witness to society has its parallel in the Roman Catholic Church [1] As a result Christianity's preoccupation with its sectarian rifts came to be challenged by a new self-image—its becoming an advocate for the power of morality to transform not only individuals but a corrupt society. The work of these religious leaders deepened and broadened their churches' understanding of their public responsibility in a variety of ways. It is a tribute to their pioneering work that today's readers confront the flood of social responsibility documents they initiated, an embarrassment of riches, which few individuals could ever hope to master. (2)

In spite of this academic ecumenical consensus which seriously seeks to address the significance of issues of justice, power, and love in today's world, the ministries of mainline churches often seem completely irrelevant. That may be due in part to what is a proper sense of modesty on their part. What difference can a local congregation make in the face of the world's social problems when its own problems of mission, if not maintenance, appear overwhelming? Communities may conclude that addressing worldly issues could prove distracting and divisive. Certainly there are both religious and cultural reasons for keeping religion disengaged from culture. Popular opinion often holds it that religious belief is purely a matter of individual interest and has no proper public role. A common religious perspective holds that spirituality is a private pilgrimage in which the individual is sovereign and operates independently from institutional religion. Both see the churches' engagement with the political order to be inappropriate if not incomprehensible. In either case, religion, although not persecuted, is ruled socially out of the game.

The privatization of religion has become a growing phenomenon particularly in most of Europe and parts of North America for quite other reasons as well. For many moderns religion is not a matter of life and death. Ultimate issues have become too difficult to deal with. Life itself has become mostly a matter of life style. That means, of course, a radical reduction in the dignity of life. In America this shift has had major cultural significance. As the culture has become more secular it has become increasingly individualistic. Thus nowadays, "private" is good while "public" is not so good. The "good life" means to live as privately as possible, to be autonomous, independent, and well-supplied with a strong sense of self-esteem—however unjustified. The not-so-good-life means living in public housing, having to go to P.S. 51 instead of to St. Bede's, and then to a community college instead of to Yale.

Transportation? Mass transit instead of a snappy BMW? Health care? Please, not socialized medicine. Hell? Other people. The presumption that the private is always better is just assumed, its just taken for granted. At its deepest level, however, it is characteristically a sign of social isolation, of the fragmentation of human life, a vague sense of disconnectedness, a personal awareness of the fragility of family life and, for many, a boredom which for some has an obvious escape: self-destructive behavior.

Parker J. Palmer's widely influential study, "The Company of Strangers," has explored the spiritual significance of this privatization of culture. He sees the root problem as a kind of pervasive myopia. We seem to have lost the ability to recognize the reality of the public for what it is. We are a part of what we do not see. We do not recognize that a fully human, productive and fulfilled life, is necessarily a life lived in public, a life among strangers. We know the strangers are all around us of course, but we generally assume that strangers are threats. Some of them may be. But we forget that our own particular threat is more likely to come from someone we know quite well, a member of our family or a former friend.

At its root public means people and therefore is inescapable. But our sense of what public means for us personally has eroded. Typically we have come to assume that public affairs means political affairs. That's a more remote and less personal matter. Most of us are certain that we want to have as little to do with politics as possible—with a possible exception once every four years. Palmer puts it clearly:

*At its most basic level, the public life involves strangers encountering each other with no political agenda at all. In fact, the public life is "pre-political." It's more basic than politics; it existed long before political institutions were developed and refined; and a healthy political process (at least, the process we call democracy) depends on the preexistence of a healthy public life. As important as it is to attempt to influence the government, it is even more important to renew the life of the public.* [3]

The excessively high value which privatization places on itself dilutes the church's spirituality and inevitably damages its understanding of its mission. Note how Parker sees it alienating the church from its own sense of vocation:

*The church preaches a vision of human unity which means very little if not acted out in the public realm. Surely that vision applies to more than family and friends. Surely it is a vision which claims more than the commonality of those who think and act and look alike. Surely that vision reaches out to include those who are alien, different, strange. If so, then the church must incarnate its vision in public, for there and only there is the stranger to be found.* [4]

If Palmer is correct, where does that leave those who hold, for whatever reason, that the church ought not get engaged deeply in public life? The New Testament makes their problem acute. Matthew's Gospel ends with Jesus charging his followers to leave lovely Galilee and go out in mission to a difficult, unfamiliar world. Did that world not have a public life? Is the world that John's Gospel says that God loves not a world at all but only a number of individuals devoid of any public culture? [5] How could anyone not notice that in both Testaments the stranger and the alien are typically portrayed as bearers of a divine blessing? [6] That should not be a surprise. Is not each of us a stranger to almost the total population of the world? Why should billions of people be afraid of you?

It is the task of both spirituality and ethics to bring some sense into this confusion. From different perspectives each alerts us to our connectedness to other human beings. Spirituality does this more radically and more inclusively since it shows how our connectedness is sacred, inescapable, and universal. Ethics appears to be more obvious since it focuses on the merely human actions, behaviors, attitudes which we employ to express ourselves. Ethics don't make us do anything in particular. It just alerts us to the sometimes unfortunate fact that whatever we do or don't do helps or harms others as well as ourselves. Understanding this fact is not as easy as it sounds. We do indeed have a right to expect to be treated fairly by others even though we do not treat them or ourselves fairly. Perhaps that's not fair, but that's why spirituality is required. It enables us to see that ethics rests on something deeper than itself.

Every social group employs all sorts of rules to indicate what behaviors are expected. But individuals and groups never fully comply with the rules they affirm. This is not mere hypocrisy. It is a recognition that every design of moral behavior rests on deeper assumptions. No group can exist without rules of behavior, stated or implicit, crude or subtle, unfair or enlightened. There is not an option for human beings to have no moral options. Whether we wish it to be this way or not, everyone is involved in the creation and violation of rules. None of us can escape participating in this joint project with other people—mostly people not of our own choosing. As Pascal might have put it, this moral destiny is a part of the grandeur and misery of what it means to be human. You can't take it or leave it. You're stuck with it. That's a part of your dignity and beauty and, of course, your de facto spirituality.

The good news today is that there appears to be growing awareness that morality is social and not merely private, that being connected is better than being isolated. Even a short list connecting human rights with human responsibilities raises major questions about that social dimension:

- *What are our rights and responsibilities for the natural environment? What are our obligations for the future of human beings and all creatures? How is the planet to be protected from being abusively exploited by commerce? How can that global responsibility be defined and politically enforced?*
- *What are our rights and responsibilities for the economic order, at home and abroad? What are the religious implications of the materialists' dogma, "I spend, therefore I am?" Since poverty is related to local structures and seems unlikely to be abolished in the near future, how can it be managed so that its dehumanizing effects can be challenged and mostly overcome?*

- *What are our rights and responsibilities for the education and health of all populations? What are the powerful domestic political forces which oppose the Constitution's emphasis on the nation's obligation to provide for the general welfare?*
- *What are our rights and responsibilities for developing democratic institutions that are effective champions for civil and human rights? How may the culture as well as the courts address traditional patterns of discrimination on the basis of age, ethnicity, gender, national origin, religious belief, and sexual orientation? Why can't our holidays become public celebrations of truth and reconciliation?*
- *What are our rights and responsibilities for the elimination of nuclear weapons and related weapons of mass destruction? What are effective ways to develop non-violent strategies for resolving international disputes? Why do popular politicians believe that war-making is more attractive than peace-building? How can religion subvert our pervasive dogmas of violence?*

The good news is not that these items are easy to deal with. Nor is it that any individual acting alone can solve even one of them. The good news is that for a significant number of people a moral agenda as expansive (or limited) as this need not be dismissed as an impossible. The point is that it is becoming increasingly recognized that it is the public's task to wrestle with issues such as these so we can work for the needed changes in attitudes and behaviors that will avert the apocalyptic consequences each portends.

That will take intelligence, patience, creativity, wisdom and cash. It will take greater measures of persistence, imagination, and hope than we ever have had to summon in the past. That does not mean that it is not possible. It does mean that we need to have robust communities which can generate interest in these kinds of questions.[7] Some of these communities are at work seeking to motivate people to love the world as God loves it. In them people are regularly called to be free and confident enough to love their neighbors as themselves. Who are these people? Some of them are reading these lines. In these communities thinking about ethics (which is humanly unavoidable) leads inevitably to thinking about spirituality, both intimate and ultimate. [8]

So far we've been looking very briefly at ethics. How about the other part of the equation, the spiritual life? That can be even more controversial. When we begin by asking what is meant by spirit, we may find that tracking some biblical spoor will be helpful. For example:

- *Spirit is primordial. In the beginning Spirit or wind (ruach) sweeps over the whole creation.* [9]
- *About 1000 BCE it was commonly believed that the Spirit of God could enter prophets so they would become vehicles of the will of YHWH. Samuel's anointing of Saul as king was coupled with an outpouring of the Spirit upon a band of "enthusiasts," dancing and singing in prophetic frenzy. Samuel ordered Saul to join in with them so the spirit of YHWH could fall on him and "turn him into another man."* [10]
- *Much later and in a different place, the priests understood the work of the Spirit in a different way. They sang of the Spirit in terms of the need for public and personal righteousness and renewal:*

> **Create in me a clean heart, O God,**
> **And renew a right spirit within me.**
> **Cast me not away from your presence**
> **And take not your Holy Spirit from me.** [11]

- *In the New Testament the Spirit is pictured as a bird that descended at Jesus' anointing. Some said that when they saw the dove they heard a twinning of prophetic and poetic voices: "You are my beloved Son; with you I am well pleased."* [12]
- *In his conversation with "Nicodemus, a leader of the Jews," Jesus seems to recall Genesis as he likens the Spirit to the wind over the waters at the creation. Without water and Spirit there can be no spiritual life. Significantly, the creative space into*

which we all are born, a mother's womb, came to mind. In his case that would have been Mary's. [13]

- John interrupts his extended account of the surpassing dignity of Jesus' passion with an unusual "spiritology." In spite of the grievous difficulties yet to come, the disciples have no reason to feel abandoned because the Spirit of truth, a divine helper and advocate, will come to guide them into all truth. It's to their advantage that Jesus will soon depart! [14]

- Fifty days later Jews "from all over the world" gathered at Jerusalem to celebrate Pentecost, a feast recalling YHWH's giving of the Law to Israel through Moses. This year, Luke says, God gave a new gift, the Holy Spirit. "Devout Jews . . .from every nation under heaven" were startled at hearing the roar of a great wind. They were probably even more surprised to hear the disciples suddenly speak in a multitude of languages from Asia, Africa and Europe. Luke admits that onlookers said the disciples were merely drunk. And so early in the day at that! Actually Luke is giving his readers here another one of his nativity stories. She is Ecclesia, the Bride of Christ they would soon call her, born to be the community of the new covenant, a community for all nations under heaven. The Holy Wind is bringing in a new creation. [15]

- Probably most first century hearers of Luke's somewhat embarrassing narrative would have quickly concluded that this disruptiveness, craziness, ecstasy is exactly what "all nations under heaven" do not have a need for. The Saul of the first century, aka Paul, thought otherwise. If anything is not nailed down, frozen in the past, fearful of the future, it is the Spirit of God. The Spirit that anointed Jesus is the Spirit of God's new creation. This Spirit is the energy that enables all humankind to participate in a new kind of life. Here spirituality and ethics are reunited. Paul sketches how this looks in his brief meditation on the fruit of the Spirit, a kind of climax to one of his earliest letters (48-49 CE). The meditation comes as something of a surprise. It follows an angry but brilliant argument against those who would turn the good news of Christ into a legal code:

> **The fruit of the Spirit
> is love, joy peace,
> patience, kindness, generosity,
> faithfulness, gentleness, self-control.
> --there is no law against these things.** [16]

So we see that even a brief overview of but one spiritual tradition can be daunting. This one certainly has stimulated a wide diversity of commentary. Much of that is confusing too. Perhaps, then, the time has come for us to try to seek simplicity. We can begin by asking if we don't want our human lives to flourish. Don't we all want to be well and, for that matter, well connected? Don't we think that we owe it to our children to show how this can work for them? What would be a spirituality that would be simple, joyful and durable for a whole lifetime? Here's one possibility:

## A BODILY SPIRITUALITY

From infancy until our dying day, we need to get clean, to get fed, and to get connected to a dependable source of love and kindness. These are essential. We share some if not all of these needs with all the other members of the animal kingdom. The biblical memory affirms each of these needs as features of what we could call a bodily spirituality. This is a celebration of the material creation as good, real and beautiful. It seeks an integration of body, mind and spirit. What we understand each of these to be and of their relationships to each other has changed and will continue to do so over time. What endures are the imperatives: Get clean, get fed, get connected to an enduring source of love and justice.

## A PROBLEM

A constant in human experience is our vulnerability to attacks on our physical, mental, and spiritual well being. Children understand this very well. Adults frequently encounter self-destructive behaviors individually and socially. We experience this destructiveness at a conscious level chiefly in terms of hostility, a separation from others as well as from ourselves and from God.

A classic formulation for this hostility is *incurvatus in se ipsum*, a being turned in on oneself, a kind of making oneself the center of the moral universe. [17] This isolation typically evokes resistance and resentment. It is experienced as a brokenness, a not-being-related to any durable goodness. Awareness of this hostility evokes anxiety which may lead to the fabrication of idols, visible or invisible--temporary alternatives for an enduring goodness. As substitutes they appear to be attractive stop-gaps. We can make and control them so that we do not have to be related to any goodness beyond ourselves.

This alienation from one's self is commonly expressed in a refusal to care for our bodily, mental, and spiritual life. Indifference to one's own need for well being validates any need to enhance the life of those to whom we are connected. It certainly can function as an unwillingness to be connected to any ultimate goodness  It is a living in the absurdity of the infantile belief: the universe exists for me!

What begins as a spiritual problem quickly infects everything. Amos resurrected would point out how this works in the twenty-first century:

- *Environmentally this hostility-as-indifference is the exploitation of nature, as a mere possession to be used for one's own material profit. Nothing is sacred but my success.*

- *Economics is not really, as is sometimes claimed, a worldly philosophy. It is mostly the rationalization for an anti-worldly morality, one which in its most popular forms provides the rationale for treating the world and most of its people with aggressively self-serving hostility.*

- *Politics, too is everywhere degraded. Instead of being a serious advocate for the well-being of the polis, it labors acidulously to provide justifications for stealing other people's land, for exploiting the disenfranchised, for rushing to war as the preferred method for furthering national economic interests.*

Alienation, hostility, anxiety, fear: no single word is adequate to capture the brokenness in human life and its communities. However, they do unite in one respect. They all refuse to recognize our interconnectedness. They all work to keep us from joining in the dance of life.

## GETTING CLEAN AND KEEPING CLEAN

Who doubts that cleanliness is necessary for physical health? [18] We are much less clear about its mental and spiritual meaning. A bodily spirituality is alert to the connections among physical, mental, and moral realities. All three need to be clean. In antiquity provision was made for public baths and public baptisms. Both forms of cleansing were celebrated and enjoyed. Getting clean was a social event. In Judaism at Qumran and at the Jordan baptisms were serious rites of spiritual cleansing. The New Testament expanded on its meaning so what is basically a very common event, a washing of the physical body, became a sign of a cleansing of all that one is. Hostility is a pollution that can be washed away when one becomes connected to Christ and to his body. [19]

The problem for spirituality is the loss of cleanliness, a serious infection by evils that separate us from others, from ourselves, and the ultimate Other. The longing to overcome those separations is understandable. That overcoming is in various ways the gift which the washing bestows. Probably there is no more immediate instance of that cleansing than the experience of forgiveness. The psychological and political implications of forgiveness are extraordinarily powerful. Who can face a single day with confidence and hope without the assurance of forgiveness for the failures of the past? What is more potent than forgiveness for healing the alienations, personal and social, that one has suffered? You haven't done anything terribly wrong that you can think of in the last few days? (Maybe you don't have a good memory. Maybe you're not aware that you've been misunderstood and caused pain without knowing about it. Maybe . . .)

But you need to know that some people don't see their moral life that way. They expect a great deal from themselves. They are interested in exploring the reach of their moral responsibility and realize that in specific areas their record it is deeply flawed. They actually stand up in public and say:

**God of all mercy, we confess that we have sinned against you, opposing your will in our lives. We have denied your goodness in each other, in ourselves, and in the world you have created. We repent of the evil that enslaves us, the evil we have done, and the evil done on our behalf . . .** [20]

Of course, one may ask who really does fully appreciate the goodness that surrounds us, that is in us? But how can we grow into it if we are not aware of this as a possibility? And then there is the evil done on our behalf and which we have benefited from. And what about the evils we have not summoned and which are greater than our power to resist them? How is the celebrated self-made person going to find the capacity to meet such challenges? Only a participation in a transcendent forgiveness that encompasses all that we know and do not know could make being able to forgive an honest possibility.

All washings, sacred and ordinary, are exercises in cleansing. So too are most prayers.

There is an ancient but well known prayer that does not mention the name of Jesus but makes the giving and receiving of forgiveness the central meaning of a community's spiritual life. The Lord's Prayer shows that divine forgiveness is conditional. "Forgive as we forgive others" can be very restrictive indeed. Equally disturbing is the prayer's consistent use of plural, not singular pronouns. For its author, prayer is a social act. Most of his followers strongly disagree with him on both of these points. [21]

The innovation cited in the Gospels' accounts of Jesus' baptism is that in his case, the washing's meaning got shifted. This washing is not a confession of sin; it is an ordination. It is an acting out of a recollection of what being a servant of God means. The act is a mission statement, a public affirmation and acceptance of an extraordinary vocation. As such it is both a moral and a spiritual event. The spiritual signs are all there: the bird, the voice from heaven, the biblical echoes. The moral significance will soon be evident: this is what the calling to love God and neighbor will be for this man.

The connection between washing and vocation may not seem obvious. But what could be more appropriate? You got to get cleaned up before you go to work. Getting clean is not narcissism, it is an act of caring. What is your work, what are you to do with your life? Is it good for nothing or is its goodness a gift to be shared? Is its personal purpose to make money so you can consume as much of the environment as possible? Or can you see your personal life as a calling, a vocation to show what loving God and neighbor can be here and now? You are not called to be a Messiah. That's been done. You have to figure out what you are called to be.

## Eating Well

Oh dear, the deer. What can you do to keep the deer from eating the flowers in your garden when you live in a big city like Washington, DC? Of course they're hungry. They have to eat. They were here before people came. Without food they and we will starve. And if the food is dangerous, that's not good news.

What is true for our bodies is also true for our mental and moral life. Eating is a very big deal. The earliest extant record of anything we have from the life of Jesus, older than any of the Gospels, is an account of the meal he hosted, actually his last meal with his followers. [22] Of course, there had been a lot of other meals before that, meals with sinners, meals with the rich, meals out of doors with very large groups of all sorts of people. And according to the Epilogue to John, there was a terrific post-resurrection breakfast on the beach not in Jerusalem but up north at the Sea of Galilee. Jesus' final dialogue with Peter gave him his new vocational charge: "Feed my lambs. Feed my sheep. Follow me." [23]

Jesus' focus on eating is an affirmation of the importance of bodily life. Hunger is not a good idea. The artistic tradition cannot imagine Jesus being overweight, but he does seem to have a great deal of interest in food. Meals were a part of his gospel, the good news of the coming reign of God. He tells a story about how an out-of-control son is welcomed home with a sumptuous banquet featuring roast veal (Marsala perhaps?), a far cry from having to eat with the pigs. John says Jesus' first miracle showed his unsuspected skill as a maker of superb wine—astonishing everyone by its quality and quantity. [24] When he taught them to pray, he said that right after praying for the coming of the reign of God, to pray for getting their physical needs met, especially food for the next day.

Hunger is not spiritually neutral. The struggle for food is also a major theme in human history—although rarely recognized as such by reasonably well fed historians. In the twenty-first century the production of food has become a global industry dominated by politically powerful corporations. While the industry has prospered financially, it fails to provide sufficient and healthy food for most people in the world. A steep increase in the prices of food and fuel prices has had an especially severe impact on the poorest in the so-called developing countries.[25] Since the agricultural-political complex has not found it commercially possible for most people to get the food they need, spiritually motivated political action groups such as Bread for the World have sprung up to serve as advocates for the hungry. Some national governments have become willing to develop globally responsible agricultural policies when they become aware that doing so not only enjoys very strong public support but is pragmatically effective as well. [26]

Food is not only a moral and political issue. It's a spiritual challenge--especially to the defective polity and piety common in Christian assemblies. In that order (a) Who gets to eat? and (b) What's going on here?

(a) *It's as though your mother had invited you to come home for Thanksgiving. All the relatives would be coming you're told. You have to come. But when you get there, it develops that there are seating problems at the table. Instead of sitting down to eat and drink together, the family spends its time in the front yard trying to determine who had the correct understanding of the menu (which, unfortunately, mother had neglected to print out ahead of time). Indeed, did the family members she had asked to help out by serving the food have the legal authority to do so? It seems that before everyone in this rather large family had arrived, most of them had decided to have as little to do with other members of the family as possible since they didn't know them well and, in fact, they didn't really respect each other. It's all so confusing. What's a mother to do?*

The story may seem unforgivably sentimental, but it is probably an understatement. For a very long time now the followers of Jesus have found that while there are not many things they can agree on, they can at least agree on this: We can not, we must not eat together. This is how their argument plays out: If we eat together, that would mean, quite literally, that we are companions. And that we are not. Some of us are qualified to eat together and some of us are not. If you do not meet the conditions which some of us have set down, we cannot eat with you. It is true that Jesus had said that his cup of a new covenant is for many and that it was intended for forgiveness. But since our knowledge of Jesus' intent is impeccable, we have no need to be forgiven for what we think is best. Anyhow since there is no evidence that the disciples themselves would be able to satisfy our requirements, it surely was a mistake for him to be so careless as to say that this cup is for many. What we need and have are polities that make sure that his many followers are not required to be companions.

(b) *The other question is what's going on here?*

Jesus' supper also was a meal of thanksgiving. There is no doubt that when he took the bread he gave thanks. There is no record of his words of institution. [27] But it is more than likely that his table prayer would have been a typical Jewish *berakah,* a blessing or benediction, an offering of praise to God whom he called Father. He praised his Father while being aware of what would likely happen to him very soon. How do you say thank you to God knowing that you, like any condemned prisoner, are about to eat your last meal?

Jesus' act of thanksgiving to God has been a part of his followers' act of remembering him. Often, however, they have not found it possible to focus with him in his own act of ultimate thanksgiving. The temptation to resist any giving of thanks can be very strong. In the last century, however, a flood of theological research has been able to sweep clear the debris of centuries which often had buried Jesus' focus, his blessing of God. [28] At present that memory is being given its central role in the worship life of all Christian communities. If this continues, Christian spirituality is on the verge of becoming again what it was for Jesus: a life of thanksgiving to God.

## Getting Connected: Staying Whole

Religion makes heavy use of the word "salvation." What does that mean? The ancient root of the English word, salvation, is the Latin *salvus,* akin to the Greek *holos,* which means "being whole." In modern times being saved has often been limited to mean either being rescued from hell or being forgiven or being liberated, etc. None of these is wrong by itself but none is fully adequate to express the inclusivity required. The word salvation itself is in need of being saved. All of these familiar aspects of salvation imply some kind of connectedness. Fragmentation is not a good idea. Being physically, mentally, spiritually whole is a wonderful idea.

We are not politically or psychologically free if we are under control of a destructive, hostile power. We are not morally healthy when we are captured by rage, fear, guilt. One way for saving the meaning of salvation would begin by recovering the inclusive range of meanings which wholeness denotes. Being physically whole is connected to being spiritually whole. Having a strong body but being psychologically depressed is not trivial: it is bad news. Being good at spiritual exercises but not having a regular discipline of physical exercise is no better. Being forgiven can be psychologically and intellectually liberating. Bodily spirituality identifies and celebrates the connections among our physical, mental, and spiritual energies.

The New Testament writers just assume that this is how salvation works. The integration of all three is central to the unprecedented claim that the word of God can and has become flesh. The vulgar bumper sticker that proclaims that "Jesus saves" is correct as an exercise in heavy duty theology: The Son of Man really is here to free us, heal us, and give us life. His bodily life is present among us in a variety of ways.

a. *He was not an angel nor a figure in a fairy tale. He was an historical figure, with a body and mind very much like the rest of us. Nineteenth century academics were fascinated by the figure of the so-called historical Jesus. Some wanted to minimize, others wanted to abolish, the elaborate Christological structures that often seemed to distort modern views of him and what he did. "Down in front," they cried. "Let's see what was really going on back there." Most of the old structures were not intended to deal with the concerns of nineteenth century Europe so it is not surprising that the theological demolition crews met with significant and easy success. Their greater achievement, from our point of view, is what was left standing after most of the dust had settled. Research scholars reached a credible consensus later shared by secular historians and non-Christian theologians alike: Yes, a man called Jesus of Nazareth really did live in first century Palestine. He would have been known as Joshua and he was killed by an obscure Roman official, Pontius Pilate. That's not quite the fullness of Christian spirituality. But without that there can be none.*

b. *In different ways the Gospels speak of Jesus' connecting his identity to that of his followers.*[29] *This does not seem to be a reward for good behavior. Nor is it an extinguishing of their particularity. The language seems metaphorical. It does not speak of bodily life as such. In time that could spring from these roots of connectedness.*

c. *We have noted that Jesus himself used the word body in a way related to but different from his concrete physical structure of bones and flesh. Before anything in the New Testament as we have it was written, the unlettered followers of Jesus insisted that in the few hours before his death, he had spoken of giving his life, himself, to them. He did this by an action: a giving of common bread which he called his body and after the meal, a giving of a cup of wine which he called the life blood of the new covenant which he had embodied.*[30] *This very strange language seemed to evoke no comment from his disciples as though what he had said was perfectly obvious. What was obvious is that his last will and testament was not a document. It was an act of giving food which henceforth would be understand to be his giving himself to his friends. They did not forget that. Did he not repeatedly say that in the future he wanted to be remembered by more meals like this?*

*d. They did remember him in this way and in so doing the image of Jesus' body took on a third, but related, meaning. The community in which Jesus' sacrificial action of giving his body, himself, to his followers was recalled. And that community itself also came to be called his body, the body of Christ.* [31] *Soon it would be claimed that this body of Christ would be present wherever his followers would be. This new body rapidly spread east into Asia, west into Europe and south into Africa. This spontaneous, disorganized mission into all the known world was understood to be God's doing, the work of God's spirit. Under extremely difficult conditions the body of Christ, no longer in a garden tomb in Jerusalem, had quickly become a world-wide phenomenon.*

*e. That is not all. With the exception of the first of these ways of speaking of the body of Christ, they all depend on what we now get to last. The resurrection of the body of Jesus is described in the texts in a wide variety of ways. They do agree that his body did not remain in Joseph's tomb. A very close disciple said she had seen Jesus after he had died, but she didn't recognize him. She thought he was a gardener. Others too said they did not recognize him either, but then when they broke bread with this stranger, they suddenly saw it was Jesus.* [32] *Yet another disciple said that he refused to believe that Jesus could still be alive. But that was just before he fell to his knees in shock and astonishment.*

It is impossible to reduce the collage of these and other reports into a single, coherent narrative. The tradition itself resists that. Yet, without belief in his resurrection, there would have been no followers of Jesus. Without the body of the historical body there could be no giving of his body to his friends at Jerusalem, Emmaus or Galilee, no communities of his body popping up all over the empire. Whether they and their billions of descendents were all deluded can neither be proved nor disproved—no matter how many times both have been attempted. Such attempts have nothing to do with the message of Easter. Proofs depend on the repeatability of the ordinary, what can be accounted for or demonstrated by comparison to similar events. Since the resurrection of Jesus is not the resuscitation of a dead man, it does not conform to the canons of ordinary, repeatable experience. It is unique and extraordinary. It is a burst of the sacred into the profane, the movement of holiness into the mundane.

The transfiguration accounts in the Gospels, often seen as proleptic visions of Easter, use a term that can give us a way of referring to this burst of sacred light into mundane life. [33] At the transfiguration, we read, there was a metamorphosis of Jesus, a change in the form of his body, so that it was possible briefly to anticipate an appearance of a body radiant in divine glory. Resurrection is a word which refers to the power of God to change the form of a human body so that in its new structure it is able to participate in his divine radiance. A continuing reality can have a variety of forms. A body can assume different shapes. They who share in the body of the risen Christ are incapable of being separated from him, his love, his light, his life. Christ is the first evidence in creation that this is what God ultimately does in his being connected to those whom he loves and who find it possible to love him This communion is what is meant by eternal life.

All these ways of speaking of Jesus' body refer to the valence of the word made flesh. Faith is living intentionally in this power. All are open to human experience:

  a. *We are all historical beings.*
  b. *We all can live between memory and hope.*
  c. *We live in communities of connection—global in extent and eternal in destiny.*

*d. Our spirituality is a living toward a future that presents an enduring life of love instead of our enduring an existence of meaningless and extinction.*
*e. We can refuse to live in a merely banal, profane world.*
*f. We can begin to live in a sacred world, a world that is within, under, and beyond all things.*

**A Wrap-up**

To speak of the courage to believe is something of an act of courage itself. Belief can mean affirming just about anything. Tyrants and fanatics are not without their fiercely held beliefs. The modern world is awash with superstition and gullibility. Multitudes of our contemporaries believe in the superiority of a particular race or national culture (always one's own, of course), or in the inevitable triumph globally of atheistic materialism, or in the natural virtue in all human beings, or in the wisdom of one's own cynicism, or in the next new thing. There is no lack of beliefs among us. So if beliefs—including believing that all beliefs are foolish—are found in all known cultures, why speak of anyone's having to have courage to be a believer? Belief, in one form or another, is inevitable.

The courage needed is not a matter of having beliefs. It lies in the particularity of belief. What needs to be included? Among the countless options available, these few pages have attempted to explore one which is currently unfashionable. They have reflected on a tradition of belief that goes back at least four millennia and is shared in significant part by three major world religions. All three see that revitalizing the primacy of justice is their major project in the twenty-first century. It is also a very personal quest for members of all three, a quest which could actually succeed since each believes it is sustained by a constant Companion who is the source of justice.

Beliefs wax and wane, grow sterile and then prove robust once more. That's true for religious beliefs as well. When belief is understood to refer to the act of reflecting on the possibility of life's meaning something, where there is the awareness that what one can know is not just an incomprehensible chaos, then we may be able to move ahead. Where it is possible to believe that life can have a logos, a logic that is greater than the thinking subject, a logos within which one is able to live into the gift of an abundant life, then the range of lively belief opens up.

The awareness that life's logos is not an invention, but is a discovery—much like suddenly seeing a star hitherto unseen by the naked eye or stumbling by accident across a poem that changes the way one understands oneself. The discovery is a gift. Its power is not an achievement which one can copyright or boast of having deserved. It is a light coming to us and enlightening us in our darkness.

These pages are but a sketch of what believing that a holy light is shining on us can mean. The light enables us to see we are connected to ourselves (body, mind, spirit) to all others (human and otherwise) and to the Ultimate Other. We are not healed by our beliefs. We are healed by the courage to believe that we can be made whole.

# ENDNOTES

## CHAPTER ONE
### The Confusions and Possibilities of Faith
1. John Barton and Julia Bowden, "The Original Story: God, Israel, and the World," (Grand Rapids: William B. Eerdmans Publishing Company, 2004), p.122
2. Op. cit. p. 119
3. Martin Luther, "The Small Catechism, The Creed, The Third Article" given in Robert Kolb and Timothy J. Wengert, eds. "The Book of Concord," (Minneapolis: Fortress Press, 2000), p. 355
4. Traditionally the years before the time of Christ have been designated as BC (Before Christ) while years after his birth have been identified as AD (Anno Domini). Style books now recommend that the former be called BCE (Before the Common Era) and the latter as CE (Common Era). This change inevitably serves to strengthen the apostolic claim that the coming of Christ is the point of reference for universal ("common") history.
5. Hebrews 11: 8-35
6. Romans 14:8

## CHAPTER TWO
### What's Real?
1. "Common Service Book with Hymnal," (Philadelphia: The Board of Publication of the United Lutheran Church in America, 1917), # 505
2. "Evangelical Lutheran Worship," (Minneapolis: Augsburg Fortress, 2006), #629
3. Genesis 1:1
4. Isaiah 6:3
5. Mark 1:15
6. Dating individual biblical books has proven controversial, but attempts at a consensus are instructive. The dates given here are from Raymond E. Brown, "An Introduction to the New Testament: The Anchor Bible Reference Library", (New York: Doubleday, 1997)
7. Genesis 50:20
8. Romans 8:18ff

9. Philemon 23
10. Psalm 22:1, 21 ff.
11. If it weren't for Matthew we would not have the Sermon on the Mount and a large number of parables, ten of which are unique to this Gospel.
12. Brown, op.cit., p. 222
13. To grasp Luke's global vision, read Acts 1:1 ff, immediately after Luke 24:53.The narrative as a whole is a journey from Bethlehem, a few miles south of Jerusalem to Rome, the center of the empire. Both volumes are dedicated to Theophilus who may have been his patron living in Greece or Syria.
14. Luke 7:33-35. J. B. Phillips, "The Gospels Translated into Modern English," (New York: The Macmillan Company, 1955) and redacted by RJE
15. Dodd, C. H., "The Interpretation of the Fourth Gospel," (Cambridge: Cambridge University Press, 1953)

## CHAPTER THREE
### What Does God Have to Do With It?

1. Martin Luther, "The Large Catechism," in Robert Kolb and Timothy J. Wengert, eds., "The Book of Concord, (Minneapolis: Fortress Press, 2000), pg. 432.
2. Douglas R. Hofstadter, "Goedel, Escher, Bach: An Eternal Golden Braid, ( New York: Basic Books, 1999)
3. Sermon on the Mount: Matthew 5:38-39, 6:24
4. Preachers have had no problem in finding homely, everyday threefold analogies on Trinity Sunday. What is time? Time is past, present and future. What is matter? Matter is solid, fluid, and gas. What is generation? Father, mother, child. Who are you? I am body, mind, and spirit.
5. I John 4:7-16
6. *Amor autem alicujus amantis est, et amore aliquid amatur.*
7. "Love is the activity of a lover, and has a certain object. Therefore, then, we have three things: the lover, that which is loved, and love." John Burnaby, trans., "Augustine: Later Works," (Philadelphia: The Westminster Press, 1955), p. 54. In this essay on "The Trinity," Augustine quickly drops his analogy because, as he immediately makes clear, it could be understood to touch on "the carnal loves of the external world." The analogy can take that risk. Note his initial sequence: the action (Spirit), the lover (Father), the beloved, (Son.) He seems to ask how can one even think of love without being, perhaps without realizing it, a trinitarian.
8. The struggles in creation, history, and the human mind are, of course, the conflict between good and evil, or, better said, between God and sin. In the

biblical record sin frequently wins. The apocalyptic literature in both Testaments addresses that problem directly. The preoccupation with the crucifixion of the Messiah in the New Testament does so even more vividly: His crucifixion appeared to be one more triumph for sin. God, however, is shown to be the real victor because the Messiah's death proved to be the death of death. God uses the disaster of his apparent defeat to be the decisive way to break the ultimate power of sin and death. It is also a foretaste of the way the history will end.

9. A major ecumenical breakthrough may have been made by a group of Finnish scholars who have shown that the traditional interpretation of Martin Luther's theology of faith has obscured his achievement. Martin consistently connects the love of God with faith in God. Faith, thus, is a participation in Christ as God's grace and God's gift (his presence). That participation is very similar, they argue, to what Orthodox theologians mean when they speak of *theosis*, divinization or glorification. See Carl E. Braaten and Robert W. Jenson, eds., (Union with Christ: The New Finnish Interpretation of Luther," (Grand Rapids: William B. Eerdmans Publishing Company, 1998)

## CHAPTER FOUR
**The First Gift**

1. I John 4:16
2. Genesis 1:1-2:3 and John 1"1-18
3. "The Song of the Three Jews," Additions to Daniel, inserted between 3:23 and 3:24 as vv 29-66 in Orthodox, Roman Catholic as well as in some Protestant Bibles as a part of the Apocrapha. It was probably inspired by Psalm 148 which it expands and is the likely inspiration for the popular Christian hymn ascribed to the patron of environmentalists, Francis of Assisi, "All Creatures, Worship God Most High!" in a new translation.
4. Matthew 5-7
5. John 1:6-8, 15
6. John 5:17
7. Martin Luther, "The Small Catechism., "Part II, The Creed in a very simple way in which the head of the household is to present it to the household," in Robert Kolb and Timothy J. Wengert, eds. "The Book of Concord," (Minneapolis: Fortress Press, 2000),. p 354 .
8. Steven C. Rockefeller and John C. Elder, eds., "Spirit and Nature: Why the Environment Is a Religious Issue," (Boston: Beacon Press, 1992). For a useful overview of the environmental perspectives of major religions see Martin Palmer with Victoria Findlay, "Faith in Conservation: New Approaches to Religions and the Environment (Washington: The World Bank, 2003).

9. New eucharistic canons place major emphasis on the creation as the first gift for which the faithful are to praise God. Cf. "Eucharistic Prayer C: God of All Power," in the 1979 Episcopal "Book of Common Prayer," p. 370 and "Thanksgiving at the Table, VII, Holy God, holy and mighty," in "Evangelical Lutheran Worship," 2006, p. 67. "The Hymnal 1982 includes 61 hymns of praise which refer to creation. ELW provides 18 hymns which focus on creation.
10. George H. Williams, "Wilderness and Paradise in Christian Thought: The Biblical Experience of the Desert in the History of Christianity & The ParadiseTheme in the Theological Idea of the University." (New York: Harper & Brothers, 1962).
11. Glenn C. Stone, "A New Ethic for a New Earth," (New York: Friendship Press, 1971)
12. For a representative sample of a variety of perspectives see the Environmental Theology Series consisting of four texts: "Baptized into Wilderness: A Christian Perspective on John Muir," "Beauty of the Lord: Awakening the Senses," Richard Cartwright Austin, "Hope for the Land: Nature in the Bible," and "Environmental Theology and Personal Ethics, (Atlanta: John Knox Press, 1988 ff.) James A. Nash's "Loving Nature: Ecological Integrity and Christian Responsibility," is a comprehensive challenge to systematic theology and ethics Ten major loci of the former are structured from an environmentalist perspective. An ethics of justice and love provide the basis for addressing environmentalist rights and responsibilities. While Juergen Moltmann's "The Future of Creation," (Phiadelphia: Fortress, 1979) deals with a wide variety of themes, his chapter "Creation as an Open System" is essential reading for scientists as well as theologians. Michael W. Fox's "The Boundless Circle: Caring for Creatures and Creation," demonstrates how as a veterinarian he understands human communion with animals to be related to an ethic of animal rights .Not all Christians are engaged in public policy formation even though in a democracy they are morally obliged to be at some level.. The Studies in Ethics volume edited by Carol S. Robb and Carl J. Casebolt "Covenant for a New Creation"(Maryknoll: Orbis and Graduate Theological Union, 1991) is a good place to begin.
13. Roderick Frazier Nash, "The Rights of Nature: A Historyof Environmental Ethics," (Madison: University of Wisconsin Press,1989)
14. Holmes Rolston, III, "Environmental Ethics: Duties to and Values in the Natural World," (Philadelphia, Temple University Press, 1988)
15. op.cit. v.
16. Bryan G. Norton, "Toward Unity among Environmentalists," (New York: Oxford University Press, 1991), p. 253
17. Robert S. Corrington, "Nature's Self: Our Journey from Origin to Spirit," Lanham: Rowman & Littlefield Publishers, Inc., 1996)

18. Arran E. Gare, ""Postmodernism and the Environmental Crisis," (London: Routledge, 1995)
19. Anthony Weston, ed., "An Invitation to Environmental Philosophy," (New York: Oxford University Press, 1999)
20. Hebrews 11:8-22, At verse 32, Barak (!) makes a fatidic cameo appearance.
21. Teilhard de Chardin, "The Phenomenon of Man," (New York: Harper & Brothers, 1959)
22. Joseph V. Kopp, "Teilhard de Chardin," (Paramus: Paulist Press, 1965)
23. Washington Post, B-10, 20 September 2008
24. Religious belief in creation as the work of God is still wide-spread in traditional cultures. When living in South Africa in South Africa in the 1970s, the writer had an academic colleague who told of a Tswana elder who told her that before the Germans came, everyone knew that *Modimo* (God) had made everything. However, now they had heard that some years ago *Modimo* had come to someplace northeast of Africa to show that he loves all people everywhere. He said, she told me, "We didn't know that."
25. The American Declaration of Independence, second paragraph, 1776
26. Langdon Gilkey, "Religion and the Scientific Future," (New York: Harper & Row, 1970), p. 11
27. With apologies to Muslims in the West and Christians everywhere
28. Karl Barth, "Church Dogmatics: A Selection," (New York: Harper and Row, 1961) pp 29-133
29. Paul Tillich, "Systematic Theology, Volume I," (Chicago: University of Chicago Press, 1951) pp. 188ff. Also "Dynamics of Faith," (New York: Harper Brothers,1957) pp 41ff and "What is Religion?" (New York: Harper and Row, 1969
30. Langdon Gilkey, "Religion and the Scientific Future," (New York:Harper and Row, 1970)
31. op.cit., p. 85
32. John Polkinghorne, "Science and Theology," Minneapolis: Fortress Press, 1998)
33. Arthur Peacocke, "Theology for a Scientific Age," (Minneapolis: Fortress Press, 1993). A comprehensive list of related publications would be a book itself. But note these few: Ian G. Barbour, "When Science Meets Religion," (San Francisco: HarperCollins, 2000; Albert Borgmann, "Power Failure: Christianity in the Culture of Technology, (Brazos Press, 2002); Francis S. Collins, "The Language of God," (New York: Simon & Schuster, 2006); Richard R. Gaillardetz, "Transforming Our Days: Spirituality, Community and Liturgy in a Technological Culture," (Crossroad, 2000); Owen Gingerich, "God's Universe," (Cambridge, MA: Harvard University Press, 2006); James E. Milller (ed.), "An Evolving Dialogue," (Harrisburg: Trinity Press, 2003); Ted Peters and Martinez Hewlett, "Can You Believe in God and Evolution?" (Nashville: Abingdon Press, 2006); Michael Ruse, "The Evolution-Creation Struggle," (Cambridge MA: Harvard University Press,

2006); Robert B. Stewart (ed.), "Intelligent Design: William A. Dembski & Michael Ruse in Dialogue," (Minneapolis: Fortress Press, 2007).
34. John Updike, "Facing Nature," (New York: Alfred A. Knopf, 1985), pp. 90-92.

## CHAPTER FIVE
### The Jesus Question
1. Mark 8:27-33
2. The classic survey of this rich tradition among early Christians is Oscar Cullmann, "The Christology of the New Testament," (Philadelphia: The Westminster Press, 1959) which focuses on Jesus as Prophet, Suffering Servant, High Priest, Messiah, Son of Man, Lord, Savior, Word, Son of God, and "designation as 'God.'"
3. Jaroslav Pelikan, "Jesus through the Centuries: His Place in the History of Culture," (New Haven: Yale University Press, 1958).His provocative list: Rabbi, Turning Point of History, Light of the Gentiles, King of Kings, Cosmic Christ, Son of Man, True (metaphysical) Image, Christ Crucified, Monk Who Rules, Bridegroom of the Soul, Divine/Human Model, Universal Man, Mirror of Eternity, Prince of Peace, Teacher of Common Sense, Poet of the Spirit, Liberator, Man for the World. A very different study not by a theologian is Richard Wightman Fox's "Jesus in America: Personal Savior, Cultural Hero, National Obsession," (San Francisco: HarperCollins, 2004) which shows why it was that among native North Americans the Roman Catholic missionaries' view of Jesus proved much more effective than that offered by the Protestants. As for a look at the future, Philip Jenkins' "The New Faces of Christianity: Believing the Bible in the Global South, (New York: Oxford, 2006) focuses on the significance of the dramatic growth of Christian churches in Africa, Asia and South America.
4. I Corinthians 1:32. "Today's English Version of the New Testament" (New York: The Macmillian Company, 1966) gives a more idiomatic translation: "offensive to the Jews and nonsense to the Gentiles."
5. The protagonist in the Book of Job is a righteous man who suffers unjustly and dares to go on to ask, "Does then the Almighty pervert justice?" At the end of this long drama during which the Deuternomic perspective is both defended and questioned, the Almighty appears on stage. Significantly, he does not side with Job's critics. But he also does not recall the significance of Israel's Covenant. In particular he even avoids answering Job's question. Instead he moves on to a brilliant meditation on the splendor of his own work, the creation of the cosmos, as set forth in Genesis 1. Surprisingly, this strategy seems to work. It moves the previously argumentative Job to a posture of deep repentance. Job's original question about the credibility of the Deuternomic theory has been explored in the drama, but Job's problem with it finally goes unanswered. Instead a new message is proposed: The

righteous are they who are humble before God. The prose framework (chapters 1 & 2 followed by the last 10 verses of chapter 44) does support the message of the Deuteronomic tradition. But the poetic drama mostly does not. Nor does it explore the equally serious related issue, "Why do the ungodly prosper?"
6. Amos 6 and 8 especially
7. Amos 2:6,7; 2:4,5; 3:1
8. Amos 9:7f. Caphtor = Crete (Europe). Kir = East of the Tigris River (Asia)
9. (2) Amos 1 and 2
10. First Song: 42:1-9, Second : 49:1-6. Third 50:40-11. Fourth 52:13-53 & 53: 1-12
11. Isaiah 53:3-6
12. Mark 16:8
13. Matthew 28:8 f.
14. Acts 2:24. Luke probably intends Peter's sermon not to be exceptional but representative of the message of the apostles.
15. Deuteronomy 21:23
16. I Corinthians 1:25. Paul's ironic comment on how the gospel exposes God's Foolishness
17. Philippians 2:6-19. Cf. Isaiah 54:22-23 and Genesis 1:29
18. An arresting exception is Acts 17:16-34 where Paul, in his mission to Athenian Gentiles, actually cites the pagan philosophers Epimenides and Aratus. (How did *they* get into the Bible?)
19. That is, they were not interested in attempting to create an objective historical reconstruction of "what really happened" in the ancient past as unrelated to their own views. To expect them to have done that would be unrealistic and, of course, anachronistic. Their purpose was not academic. It was to proclaim a new vision of God's justice. The Gentile Luke approached the Hebrew Scriptures with the same reverence, intent and effect as his Jewish colleagues. He probably had previously been a convert to Judaism.
20. Richard Bauchham, "God Crucified: Monotheism and Christology in the New Testament," (Grand Rapids: Eerdmans Publishing Co., 1998) p. 47
21. In Isaiah 52:13-53:12:12 the writer had seen that suffering is not simply God's punishment of someone who deserves it. It is certainly not an act of gratuitous violence. And above all suffering is not the end of his servant's destiny. The Hebrew tradition had declared, "The servant shall be exalted and lifted up and shall be very high." The poem Paul cites addresses the issues the prophets (and that other poet, Job) had found in the Deutronomic theological tradition. Of course the righteous need to be victorious if God is to be just. God's justice sometimes does come in our natural life time however. The earth is not heaven. God's reign is only partially realized around us and in us. The whole creation, in fact, is groaning and in travail waiting with eager longing for freedom from its bondage to decay waiting for the redemption of our bodies. (Romans 8: 18-25) What could that mean?

22. Isaiah 45:23f.
23. Isaiah 45:22. Paul repeatedly cites Israel's Scriptures as his authority for global mission: See Romans 9:15; 9:25,26. 10:18-20; 11:8-10; 15:9-12. Thus the problem of Amos, resolved by Second Isaiah, becomes a job description for Paul and other Jewish Christians. The global, inclusive, non-ethnic vision of Israel's prophets comes to be understood as YHWH's intention.
24. Baukman, p. vii
25. Identity can have a variety of meanings. In theology, other humanities, and the social sciences it is now commonly used to mean "an awareness of personal self continuity" and not merely existence.

## CHAPTER SIX
## From Moses to Martin

1. In Hebrew thought, persons' names express their identity. Cf. Exodus 3:13-15
2. Exodus 3:1-12
3. Deuteronomy 6:4-5. Statutes and ordinances dealing with the command's ethical and liturgical implication are stated in great detail in the following chapters.
4. Cf. Psalm 51:10
5. Leviticus 19:18
6. John 15:12
7. Exodus 33:11
8. While the word "righteous" is traditional, it has become somewhat pejorative in vernacular speech, sometimes being confused with "self-righteous." "Justice" is less confusing but has an academic flavor which can be restrictive and impersonal.
9. The word "salvation" has a wide range of meanings: justification, deliverance, protection, freedom, renewal, healing, life, etc. Paul probably meant it "eschatologically," i.e., an expectation or destiny to participate in God's future which is already partially present.
10. Chapters 9-11 celebrate God's faithfulness to Israel, "the children of the promise." Chapters 12-15 are ethical reflections and exhortations followed by travel plans, a large number of personal greetings, and a blessing.
11. Romans 8:18-24
12. Romans 8:38-39

13. Mark Twain, "The Adventures of Huckleberry Finn," ( New York: Literary Classics of the United States. Dist. by Penguin Books, 1982.)
14. Twain's account of the conflict of the conflict between different ways of understanding justice, the conventional (you'll be punished if you don't do what you're told is right) versus the demand of conscience (do what's right regardless of the punishment you should get) is, of course, a critique of the former. It is more than that however. Huck's willingness to be damned for doing for what he knows to be right implies that Twain was aware of the classic Christian affirmation of vicarious suffering's having liberating power. Liberation can demand a heavy cost.
15. The story of how the meaning of the exodus event was understood by modern Namibians to have been recapitulated in their struggle against the Republic of South Africa is given in Roy J. Enquist, "Namibia: Land of ears, Land of Promise," London and Toronto: Associated University Presses, 1990).
16. Martin Luther King, Jr.'s autobiographical "Stride toward Freedom: The Montgomery Story (San Francisco: Harper San Francisco. 1986) is a graphic description of how his strategy of political non-violence proved effective.

# CHAPTER SEVEN
## On Being Well and Being Well-Connected

1. John A. Coleman, "One Hundred Years of Catholic Social Teaching," (Maryknoll: Orbis Books, 1991)
2. Particularly influential have been works by John Howard Yoder, "The Priestly Kingdom: Social Ethics as Gospel," (South Bend: Notre Dame Press, 1984) and Stanley Hawerwas, "A Community of Character: Toward a Constructive Christian Social Ethic," (South Bend: Notre Dame Press, 1981). The Rauschenbusch tradition is well represented in Gary Dorrien, "Soul in Society: The Making and Renewal of Social Christianity," Minneapolis: Fortress Press, 1995. The Niebuhrian influence is clear in Glen Tinder, "The Political Meaning of Christianity: the Prophetic Stance," (San Francisco:HarperSanFrancisco, 1991). A Lutheran text is Robert Benne, "The Paradoxical Vision: A Public Theology for the Twenty-first Century," (Minneapolis: Fortress Press, 1995). A progressive evangelical voice is Brian D. McLaren, "Everything Must Change: Jesus, Global Crisis, and a Revolution of Hope," (Nashville: Thomas Nelson, 2007). An important social science study is Barry A. Kosmin and Seymour P. Lachman, "One Nation under God: Religion in Contemporary Society," (New York: Crown

Publishers, 1993). The ecumenical journal, "The Christian Century," http//www.christiancentury.org, is indispensible.
3. Parker J. Palmer, "The Company of Strangers: Christians and the Renewal of America's Public Life, " (New York: Crossroad, 1995)
4. Op. cit.
5. Matthew 28:19. John 3:16
6. Genesis 18:1-15, Ruth, Jonah, Matthew 2:1-6, Luke17:11-19, Luke 24:11-35, John 4:1-42 and 20:15. Hebrews 13:12, etc.
7. Yesterday while serving as a priest at a major cathedral, the writer was asked after the Eucharist by a Hindu from India to pray for her. Immediately following the prayer, she introduced her husband, a German Roman Catholic physicist. A spirited "science and spirituality" conversation quickly ensued.
8. It may be hard to believe, but this "which comes first, law or gospel problem" has proved painfully divisive among Protestant theologians. All agree that morality and spirituality are inseparable. But which comes first? In Wittenberg they said law and gospel. In Geneva they said gospel and law. The theological and cultural consequences of the decision has proven highly influential in nations where either confession has been dominant. The former has encouraged quietism, the later Puritanism. After centuries of dispute, it seems clear that both traditions have strengths and weaknesses. Ecumenism is encouraging each to stress its strengths and repair its weaknesses.
9. Genesis 1:2
10. I Samuel 10:5-6 and 19:18-24
11. Psalm 51:10-11. The interfaith significance of this text cannot be overestimated. It is particularly prominent in the penitential liturgies of the churches. Note too the neat and theologically important Hebraic parallelism connecting the divine and human spirits.
12. Psalm 2:7 and Isaiah 42:1
13. John 3:1-10.
14. John 14:15-31; 15:26; 16:4b-15
15. Acts 2:1-36
16. Galatians 5:22-23. As for the anger, Paul and Jesus, unlike many later Christians, believed that anger is not only ethically appropriate at times, but morally necessary. One of Paul's disciples counseled, "Be angry, but do not sin." (Ephesians 4:26) How can there be moral or spiritual growth if what is unethical does not meet resolute, even fierce opposition? The sin lies rather in not being angry in the presence of "man's inhumanity to man"—be it apathetic or deliberate. Note too the ironic touch in the list line. What Paul is commending is a far more rigorous discipline than that any code of law, religious or cultural, could ever impose.
17. This is the reformers understanding of the moral meaning of "original sin."
18. The Japanese build this into their language. *Kirei desu* can be translated either as "It is beautiful" or "It is clean."

19. The decisive text for all churches is "Baptism, Eucharist, and Ministry," (Geneva: World Council of Churches, 1982. Note especially the Introduction and pages 2-7. A helpful related study is 'Eucharistic Piety—A New Experience of Christian Community' in Wolfhart Pannenberg, "Christian Spirituality," (Philadelphia: The Westminster Press, 1983)
20. The Holy Eucharist, Washington National Cathedral, 8 March 2009
21. Matthew 6:12. "And forgive us our debts as we also have forgiven our debtors" and Luke 11:4 "And forgive us our sins as we forgive everyone who is indebted to us" have slightly different meanings, but in both cases it is the disciples' act of forgiving someone else which is the model for the measure of forgiveness God is to give them. This is the opposite of the usual saying, "Forgive others as God has forgiven you." Does Jesus' version make a difference in what forgiveness costs us?
22. I Corinthians 11:23-34. This letter was probably written about 54 CE and the passage here refers to an earlier oral tradition. This pre-Pauline tradition is the earliest witness we have for the central event in distinctively Christian worship.
23. John 21:1-19
24. John 2:1-11
25. Todd Post's Bread for the World Background Paper, "Global Development: Charting a New Course" states, "Years of bad policy choices are at least partly to blame for the sudden spike in (food and fuel) prices. While developed countries were protecting their farmers—paying subsidies that undercut farmers in poor countries, maintaining high tariffs to keep imports out, imposing export bans to protect their own food supply—the agricultural sector in many developing countries was devastated. Developing countries that were once self-sufficient producers of their own food became net food importers. More recently, policies in rich countries have encouraged their farmers to divert crops away from food production into biofuels." This 26. The Pew Forum on Religion and Public Life 2008 report on "The Government and Needy Americans" showed that "a comfortable majority of people . . .support more government help for hungry and poor people." E.g.: The government should do more to help needy Americans, even if it means going deeper into debt: 62% of the population. Government today can't afford to do much more to help the needy: 29%Neither/Both: 5%.Don't Know/Refused:4%. Op. cit. p. 8.
27. There is no record of words of institution for the meal in any of the texts. Maybe there were none. The tradition does recall words of distribution, however, but that served a different purpose. Background Paper

was published by Bread for the World in Washington, DC in December 2008. Cf. (www.bread.org)
28. See note 19 above especially pages 10-17.
29. Matthew 25:40-46 and John 14-17.
30. I Corinthians 11:24. Mark 14:22-25. Matthew 26:26-29. Luke 2:15-20.
31. I Corinthians 12:12-13:13. Ephesians 1:23
32. Luke 24:13-35
33. Mark 9:2-8. Matthew 17:1-13. Luke 9:28-36. The Greek *metemorphothe* is usually translated as transfigured.